Mighty Messianic Prophecy:
Biblical Research of Predictions Proving that Jesus Is God

Written, illustrated, and published by Joe Chiappetta

Copyright 2015 by
Joe Chiappetta
6301 N. Sheridan Road, Unit 22L
Chicago, IL 60660

www.joechiappetta.blogspot.com

Proofreader: Denise Chiappetta

ISBN: 978-0-9644323-8-3

Table of Contents

Mighty Messianic Prophecy:
Biblical Research of Predictions Proving that Jesus Is God

By Joe Chiappetta

Chapter 1: Lost in the Future or Anchored to the Ancient Book

Do you know your maker? For too much of my life, I would sadly have to answer that question with a definitive "No" or "Not really," or even "Get out of my face!" Looking back, I must admit that my seeking of truth was quite pathetic. Fiction and fantasy were more to my liking back then. Serious and disciplined research into the truth was considered unattainable. In fact, my fictions and fantasies were more real to me than the truth. I could tell you how Spiderman got his dangerous black costume (in Marvel's *Secret Wars*), yet had no clue how to remove the dark stains of my sin from the depths of my soul.

However all that changed in 1998 when I became a follower of Jesus Christ. The dark stains have been washed away by the blood of Jesus in the waters of my baptism. I am so grateful to be able to know God through living out a new life by his word. This is largely thanks to some dear old neighbors of mine, the Shelbrack family, as well as an amazing woman named Denise (whom I later married). These valiant few so courageously reached out to me by sharing their faith and their lives that even to this day, I still know my maker. My maker is the Messiah, and the Messiah, as we shall see from studying the Bible, is Jesus. And Jesus, as we shall see from research into prophecy, is God.

Other peoples and nations can go on inventing all sorts of bizarre origins of species that may dazzle the masses for a time. Yet time is fleeting. And I choose to remain grounded in the truths of my maker, my Messiah. I hope that you will join me.

So many people from around the world that I run into here in Chicago are still like I used to be. They don't know their maker and are doing very little to get to know him, due to an ignorance or lack of faith. A few years ago, my wife and I ran into some graduate students from China who said that they had never prayed at all to anyone in their entire lifetime. One of them even thought that Easter was simply about the Easter Bunny. Not only did they not know their maker, but they didn't even think they had a maker.

Thankfully, the Bible says in Romans 10:17 that **"faith comes from hearing the message, and the message is heard through the word of Christ."** So we studied the Bible with those students and got into their lives. Within a few months' time, they became disciples of Jesus Christ--all five of them. Therefore, there is true hope for us all, no matter what might have been lacking from our upbringing.

So much about God's message to us comes alive on a deeper level when we gain greater understanding about the Messiah. We will look at who the Messiah is, what the word "Messiah" means, how active the Messiah is throughout the Scriptures, how interconnected the Messiah and God really are, and what we should be doing about all this.

Sadly, regarding those dear Chinese graduate students previously mentioned, all five of them walked away from the faith almost as quickly as they came to it. Some of the reasons for this was because they got distracted by **"the desire for other things"** (Mark 4:19), and never deepened their initial understanding of how amazing Jesus is. Messianic prophecy is one way to connect with a richer appreciation for who Jesus is, and what he has been doing all along. The more I discover about the master plan of the Messiah, the more I desire to have relationship with him as the master planner.

There are 2.2 billion self-proclaimed "Christians" in the world according to the Pew Research Center's 2015 report: *The Future of World Religions: Population Growth Projections, 2010-2050.* That's almost one third of all people on the planet. Yet would anyone believe that one out of every three people could pick up a Bible and quickly direct a person to verses that prove that Jesus is the Messiah? Don't bet your life on it.

While the rest of the world chases after non-eternal knowledge, entertainment, selfish ambition, and all sorts of idols, we will build our faith in our maker through the role of his anointed one. That is actually the literal translation of what Messiah means: anointed one. I am amazed at the amount of people--both in and out of the church-- who don't know this. Yet the significance of knowing the anointed one is literally life-changing.

To illustrate the direction our society is heading in, imagine this family scene, perhaps from the not too distant future. A father and son are lounging around in their high-tech living room while the son opens up an old and dusty box. Brittle, acidic cardboard gives off the stale odor of mildew as it permeates out from the yellowing container. The father is surprised at what his son has discovered in this long-forgotten box.

Glancing up from his fully immersive virtual reality goggles, the dad declares, "Wow that's a real authentic book! We should read it." The father is referring to the top book in the box which his son grabs in curiosity. The title of this giant vintage book evokes a sense of respect and awe: *The Holy Bible.*

6

The son, being only accustomed to multimedia eBooks, movies, virtual reality, and multiplayer online video games, has never seen an actual printed book. So, with sincerity, the boy asks "Where is the start button?"

A FATHER LOOKS UP FROM HIS VIRTUAL REALITY GOGGLES TO FIND HIS SON RUMMAGING THROUGH A BOX OF OLD ITEMS, LONG FORGOTTEN.

SILLY DADDY: LOST IN THE FUTURE

Wow, that's a REaL AUTHENTIC BOOK! WE SHOULD READ IT.

THE HOLY Bible

Joe Chiappetta

This Side Up

BUT WHERE IS THE START BUTTON?

This allegorical scene representing the increasingly aloof attitude that our world has for the Bible has led me to a significant observation; more and more, I find that people, myself included, can be easily captivated by the allure of anything new: Google Glasses, Tablets, Smartphones, Smartwatches, 3D Printers, Mini-Drones, Video Game Systems, Personal Health Tech Gadgets, the list goes on.

Who can deny a certain fascination with the development and progress of such toy-like technology and the new content that these formats pave the way for? It's hard to compete with the consumer electronics industry, which has been bringing in over $200 billion in revenue annually since 2012. Reporting this, the Consumer Electronics Association projects these numbers to increase to $214 billion in 2015. To appreciate how much money $200 billion is, consider this; you can feed over 22 million poor people with 3 meals per day for a year by spending $8 per meal. That's more people than reside in the entire population of the State of New York.

Yet people must have their new gadgets, and for too many, gadgets have replaced God. While the facade of spinning everything new as supremely better remains part of our societal value system, one ancient book continues to hold up low tech content that, despite being quite old, **"is perfect, reviving the soul,"** as stated in Psalm 19:7. That book, of course, is The Holy Bible.

As we enjoy a sense of newness in life which God allows us to have, and as we search for the next big thing, I am reminded that what really counts is for us to meditate on God's law, **"day and night"** (Psalm 1:2). Think deeply and repeatedly about what God calls us to be and to do. Most people might scoff at this kind of talk. I know this for sure, since I was such a person for three dark decades of my life.

Nevertheless, a few faithful believers, anchored to the past that was transformed by Jesus Christ on the cross, will find excitement in God's ability to **"revive the soul."** No one but God can do such a thing as to revive our inner life essence--our soul. Yet for God, that is his main line of work! Luke 19:10 explains that Jesus **"came to seek and to save what was lost."** Being a former lost soul, and completely undeserving of any sort of revival, I am so grateful that

8

God still called me to him. I was a lost cause, drunk on the future glory of self and fellow man, without a clue as to which way was up. Yet I was revived, converted, and found--only by the grace (undeserved favor) of God.

In the future, which seems to be here today and full of tantalizing distractions, our population will become increasingly polarized about God. You can even see it happening now; praying outside of home or place of worship has become taboo in a world striving to be so politically correct that prayer has been kicked to the curb. The multitudes continue to reduce time spent talking to God in favor of the many modern-day idols. Meanwhile, a select few will find an anchor for their soul in the promise of salvation through Jesus Christ, as highlighted in Hebrew 6:19, **"We have this hope as an anchor for the soul, firm and secure...."**

Therefore the following core question is left as a friendly warning, and as a challenge; are you lost in the future or anchored to God's word? Accurately predicting the coming of Jesus Christ, the Bible may be an ancient book, but it is the only book that has stood the test of time. In the end, the Bible will also be the only book to remain.

If you need help finding the *start* button, messianic prophecy is an amazing place to begin.

Chapter 2: Will the Real Scriptures Please Stand Up?

Most of my life, the topics that I have researched and written about passionately often get started because I had become alarmed or surprised about a particular issue that had previously caught me off guard. Such is the case with this study of Scriptures having to do with Jesus.

First of all, I became quite surprised when I looked up the meaning of the word "Scripture" in Thayer's Greek Lexicon, which is a historical Bible dictionary that attempts to define words as they were used at the time of their writing. Like most people, I assumed that the word "Scripture" had always and only meant what it has come to mean today: the holy writings from God. Yet I was completely wrong.

Most of the word's usage in ancient Greek literature is not dependent on any supernatural being authoring that which had been written. Used 51 times in the New Testament, the Greek word for "Scripture" is "graphe," and it simply means "a writing," or "a thing written." From Sophocles, the ancient Greek playwright (496 BC) on down the line, the same Greek word, "graphe" has been used to mean "writing." It originally started out to mean any kind of writing:

legal documents, historical accounts, letters, and of course, the recorded words of God.

This can best be seen by using the Perseus Digital Library at www.perseus.tufts.edu. This is an online database cataloging most of the surviving Greek works of antiquity. I have found it to be an amazing resource to research word origins from Greco-Roman times. As a project of Tufts University, their database is currently free to use.

Running the word "Scripture" (translated from "graphe") through the Perseus Digital Library was quite an eye opener. As an example of the word graphe's everyday usage from 431 BC, see this line from The Peloponnesian War by Thucydides (book 1, chapter 129, verse 1). "This was all that was revealed in the **writing**, and Xerxes was pleased with the letter. He sent off Artabazus, son of Pharnaces, to the sea with orders to supersede Megabates, the previous governor in the satrapy of Daskylion, and to send over as quickly as possible to Pausanias at Byzantium a letter which he entrusted to him; to show him the royal signet, and to execute any commission which he might receive from Pausanias on the king's matters, with all care and fidelity."

The word translated as "writing" in the first sentence is "graphe" in Greek. Of course, "graphe" is the same word also translated into English as "Scripture." Yet clearly, the context is merely political correspondence through letters, not godly communication. So what is going on here? What is Scripture?

I began to wonder what many people might start to wonder; when did the word "Scripture," which originally just referred to "writing" come to mean "writing from God?" After long hours looking through ancient Greek books, letters and laws, it became clear that the works of ancient Greeks like Sophocles and Plato held no clues to some sort of transitional meaning for when the word known now as "Scripture" gradually changed into exclusively meaning "the writings from God."

Therefore, I came to a simple conclusion. There is little transitional use of the word "graphe" because writings are writings. Nevertheless, the New Testament writers, inspired by God, were basically so excited about God's word that all other writings were typically insignificant to even mention.

I liken this to a few decades ago when I was poor and could only afford to make a sandwich composed of bread with nothing but potato chips in the middle. Now fast forward to the present day where my wife makes delicious veggie burgers from scratch that could easily sell for top dollar in any restaurant. Putting down the sorely lacking sandwich of chips today, I would scoff and say "That's no sandwich. This is the sandwich!" as I held up my wife's homemade veggie burger.

How does that relate to the word now known as "Scripture?" It's as if "graphe," when used to refer to writings from God, had been commandeered for the new plan that God was unfolding. All other writings are simply not in the same league as the prophetic blossoming of God's written rescue plan.

Romans 4:3 portrays the confidence which was put into God's own words. **"What does the Scripture say? 'Abraham believed God, and it was credited to him as righteousness.'"** This could equally be translated as such; "What does the writing say?" The New Testament writers don't have to specify which writing they were referring to. They were writing to believers who knew the only writing that really mattered was God's writing.

This is the case every time the word "graphe" is used in the New Testament. It always refers to God's inspired word even though the literal word by itself simply means "writing." See 2 Timothy 3:16. **"All Scripture is God-breathed and is useful..."** Even though literally this sentence could be translated as "All writing is God-breathed," no one would accept that Paul is referring to all writings from any writer. Rather, the implication is that every prophetic statement delivered from God to man is from the very mouth of God. The context makes all the difference. For a special purpose, God set aside (made holy) the writings that told his message. This is confirmed in 2 Timothy 3:15, where the context is **"the holy Scriptures,"** which Timothy had been taught from infancy. In other words, the writing in the Bible is set aside for a special purpose. Indeed, no other book is **"living and active,"** (Hebrews 4:12) except for the Bible. That's beyond special--that's the amazing authorship of God.

In similar form, consider what Timothy was told by Paul in 2 Timothy 4:2. **"Preach the Word...."** No one asks "Which word?" It is already understood that "the word," translated from "logos" in Greek, refers to a collection of things which are put together in thought, gathered together in the mind, and are expressed in words. That's Thayer's Greek Lexicon definition of "logos." Words spoken by whom, you might ask? Spoken by Christ, of course, not that Christ is part of the original ancient Greek definition of "logos" but everyone knows from reading the rest of Paul's letter that the context is Christ. Therefore Paul is commanding Timothy to preach the collected sayings and thoughts of Jesus. That, of course, must bring us to the Bible--the written word of God.

God's word (logos) is so important, that God even commandeers the meaning of logos and turns it into a proper name for the Messiah in Revelation 19:13, **"He is dressed in a robe dipped in blood, and his name is the Word of God."** This, of course, refers to Jesus, who is also named **"King of Kings and Lord of Lords,"** a few verses later (Revelation 19:16) with writing **"on his robe and on his thigh."**

When God talks about his word, and his writing, all other writing pales by comparison. After all, God, through his prophets and apostles, has revealed with the completion of the Bible, his complete plan for our lives. It is centered on his coming in the flesh as the anointed one (the Messiah) who loves us, died for us, and rose from the dead so that we too might live a new life in Christ (Christ is Greek for Messiah, which means "anointed one" in Hebrew).

In the case of the word "Scripture," by the time the Bible got translated into English, the translators created a new English word for this phenomenon of God bringing holy writings to his people. The word origin of "Scripture" according to Oxford Dictionaries supports this view: "Middle English: from Latin scriptura 'writings', from script- 'written', from the verb scribere."

The best Bible verse to demonstrate how the word "Scripture" originally just meant "writings" is in Matthew 26:56. **"'But this has all taken place that the *writings* of the prophets might be**

fulfilled.' Then all the disciples deserted him and fled." The word that English translators portray here as "writings" is "graphe." The reason they translate it as "writings" and not "Scriptures" is because the English speaking world already understands that Scriptures are writings from prophets. Therefore the phrase in English would be redundant to say "the Scriptures of the prophets." So in this case, the translators use the more historical translation of "graphe" by calling the writings what they literally are: writings.

As we focus on the Scriptures, the writings from God through the prophets, we will pay attention to the Scriptures that show us who God is, and what we need to do about it. While not the most trending topic of today's distracted world, studying messianic prophecies will get you exactly what you need to know: who God is, and what you need to do about it. Messianic prophecies are promises from the Bible. Promises in the Old Testament turn into facts about the Messiah in the New Testament--facts that define the very nature of God, and facts that should change your life, unless you're too tired to stand up for what is right in this dark world.

In Acts 2, the Israelites were remarkably attentive to the details of the Apostle Peter's message at the Feast of Pentecost during 33 AD. But why? It involved more than the miraculous tongues of fire that God had delivered to get the people's attention. The first part of Peter's sermon was a sobering truth about the death of the Messiah. Who killed the great king we've been waiting for all our lives? You did. Statements like Peter's should move you to stand straight up in grief and urgency.

Acts 2:23 **"This man was handed over to you by God's set purpose and foreknowledge; and you, with the help of wicked men, put him to death by nailing him to the cross."**

That's a big deal. Imagine all your life hearing about a hero that has been promised to be sent to rescue you. But then you find out that this hero has been killed and what's even worse: you are responsible! That is what was going on in Acts 2. But Jesus isn't your average hero. He rose from the dead--just like he said he would all along!

Matthew 16:21 **"From that time on Jesus began to explain to his disciples that he must go to Jerusalem and suffer many**

14

things at the hands of the elders, chief priests and teachers of the law, and that he must be killed and on the third day be raised to life."

What is so amazing is that this occurrence was not just predicted a few years before it happened. It was prophesied about hundreds, and even over a thousand years beforehand.

From Genesis to Revelation, these are the writings (Scriptures) to be reckoned with. Accept no substitute--no boastful words of men. Only the Bible contains verifiable statements that all came true about our God in the flesh and our God in heaven. A careful study of the Bible reveals that they are one and the same. These are the Scriptures--the only writings--that stand straight up in the name of truth. Examine them and do likewise: stand straight up in the name of Jesus--**"the way and the truth and the life."** (John 14:6)

Chapter 3: From Defective to Faithful Footing

It was a typical Men's Midweek Service in the church one Wednesday evening. Despite the cold Chicago winter, the brothers were fired up, the singing was powerful and the fellowship was all a buzz about our God. But as the Bible lesson started, something that was more than a footnote happened to me.

While moving to the other side of the room to get a better spot to listen to the sermon, a sudden stream of reddish dirt began to spray outward from below me. Obviously, one of the other brothers must have tracked in a giant clump of mud from outside and now I just stepped in it. Don't these guys have the decency to wipe their feet before they come in from the cold?

I came to this conclusion quickly and naturally. It couldn't possibly be me, since I wore clean winter boots from home. From my car to the building there was only white snow and salty pavement.

But then I took another step, which sprayed even more dirt across the floor. It began to look as if a football player had stomped his filthy cleats out along the ground. Yet this was unnervingly eerie: I was certain my boots were clean, so where on earth could this odd reddish dirt becoming from? A closer look revealed that the reddish material emanating from beneath me was unlike any mud a man could step in. Its appearance was finer than sand, yet mixed with pebble-sized uneven clumps of... who knows what. Suddenly people were starting to look at me funny. I quickly scampered toward a new spot but almost tripped over my own foot along the way.

Totally dumbfounded, I looked down at my right shoe to find that the entire sole of my extra thick winter boot had flopped out unevenly from the rest of the footwear. The bottom inch of this right boot had mysteriously ripped away from the rest of my foot, creating a wobbly mess that was spraying the fine red powder in odd directions across the floor.

Gratefully, there was a garbage can exactly where I had plopped down to listen to the sermon. Discreetly as possible, I threw the ripped sole away. Yet I could not escape the trail of red dirt that still emanated from the new bottom of my right boot. Every move I made resulted in more mess. So I tried not to move. After careful examination, it was clear that the new bottom of my boot had somehow lost all its flexibility and had transformed into a crusty deposit of dark red rubber powder.

Even with that understanding, I couldn't help but wonder; "What is going on here? Is God trying to tell me something? What is it? Is this some sort of warning message from the Lord?"

I wasn't sure. So, like a good Christian, I tried to focus on the lesson being preached--while moving as little as possible.

A baptism took place immediately after the lesson, so all the men walked across the room to gather around the water tub. As we went, I also wondered if anyone noticed that I was walking funny. Wearing an uneven right shoe one inch lower than the other shoe made me sort of hobble over to the baptism. And immediately after our new brother got out of the water, my left foot began to flop just like the other foot. I looked down, and sure enough, now both bottoms of my boots had mysteriously been ripped from the bottoms of my poor feet. Inevitably, this spawned a whole new crop of red rubber powder. Everywhere I stepped became a mist of red debris.

These strange happenings abruptly shortened me by an inch and fixed my hobbling problem. But later, while sweeping up my red trail of confusion, I again began to wonder; "What can a man possibly learn from losing both of his shoe soles in one night at church? Am I being prompted to take off my footwear because the place I am standing on is holy ground? Or was this some sort of coded prophecy? Should I repent before I lose the very footing from beneath me?"

After a score of wild interpretations, I finally came to my senses and figured it out. Repentance is always good. But God has no need for me to infuse extra meaning into defective shoes. Rather, he calls me--and you--to look for true meaning in prophecy that has an eternal impact. I am talking about messianic prophecies: real documented events in the life of Jesus. These happenings were directly alluded to or specifically predicted hundreds of years before they actually happened.

Before we go back in time again to explore more examples of these predictive events, we need to pose some questions, define some terms, and set a goal.

Messianic Questions

I have some questions for you about the Messiah. These are important questions to ask yourself now, and every day. Take note of how many you can answer with certainty:

- Who is the Messiah?
- How important is the Messiah?
- Are you excited about the Messiah now, or just at some long-gone point from your past?
- Whose Messiah is he?
- How will the Messiah impact the world?
- How will the Messiah impact you?
- Do you know the Messiah?

Prophecy Ponderings

I also have some questions about prophecy:

- What is prophecy?
- How important is prophecy?
- How will prophecy impact the world?
- How will prophecy impact you?
- Are you fluent in prophecy?

- Have you memorized any prophecy?

If you are not rock solid with your answers to these questions, this lesson will help you to mature in your understanding. Now perhaps you may be thinking, "Oh, yes, I pretty much know all that stuff. I've heard it all before."

Great, but shouldn't these truths still inspire you? Or is there an expiration date on the freshness of God's word to you? Surely not! Moreover, can you sit toe to toe with an unbeliever, or even a new Christian, and explain these prophetic concepts to them intelligently by using the Scriptures? This lesson will give you tools to help yourself and others gain a deeper appreciation for God's consistent plan.

Definitions of Biblical Terms

Prophecy (noun). Source: *Merriam-Webster Dictionary*

1) An inspired utterance of a prophet

2) The function or vocation of a prophet; specifically the inspired declaration of the divine will and purpose

3) A prediction of something to come

Prophetic (adjective). Source: *Merriam-Webster Dictionary*

1) Of, relating to, or characteristic of a prophet or prophecy

2) Foretelling events: predictive

3) That which is revealed by God

Messiah (noun). Source: *A Concise Dictionary of the Hebrew Bible* by James Strong

Strong's Reference # 4899: mashiyach

"Anointed: usually a consecrated person (as in king, priest, or saint)"

Basically the word "Messiah" means anointed one, one rubbed with oil, as in a king anointed with oil. The Greek word for anointed is Christ. By association in Scripture, the anointed one is the savior and redeemer. This, of course, is the role and title for Jesus of Nazareth.

Keep in mind that the Hebrew word for "Messiah" (mashiyach) is used in the Old Testament 39 times. In the New Testament, the word "Messiah" occurs 68 times. Additionally, the Greek word "Christ," which means "Messiah," occurs in the New Testament 469 times. That's a total of 576 times. Clearly if we want to understand Jesus, we must pay greater attention to Jesus' special title and the anointed activity going on in the Bible.

Now today, if I came over to you and poured oil on (anointed) you in this very moment, how would you take it? At the very least, you'd wonder why I was trying to mess up your hair, or ruin your favorite shirt. In fact, when I get olive oil on my neckties while eating pasta or a sandwich (which happens all too often), I sometimes have to throw those hopelessly stained articles of clothing away. But as Adam Clarke writes in his commentary (page 37) of *The New Testament* (1817) anointing was no accidental spill. "...In ancient times, prophets, kings, and priests were anointed with oil." This was a great honor from days bygone.

In Psalm 133:1-2, the precious nature of oil anointment is poetically portrayed in the anointing of Moses' older brother Aaron. **"How good and pleasant it is when brothers live together in unity! It is like precious oil poured on the head, running down on the beard, running down on Aaron's beard, down upon the collar of his robes."**

In the case of the first kings of Israel, the kings were anointed by the prophet Samuel as a sign that God was with them and chose them specifically to lead. See the anointing of King Saul in 1 Samuel 10:1 as well as the anointing of David in 1 Samuel 16.

It should not be surprising then that Jesus, the king of kings, also was anointed in Mark 14:3-9. **"While he was in Bethany, reclining at the table in the home of a man known as Simon the Leper, a woman came with an alabaster jar of very expensive perfume, made of pure nard. She broke the jar and poured the perfume on his head. Some of those present were saying indignantly to one another, 'Why this waste of perfume? It could have been sold for more than a year's wages and the money given to the poor.' And they rebuked her harshly. 'Leave her alone, 'said Jesus. 'Why are you bothering her? She has done a beautiful thing to me. The poor you will always have with you, and you can help them any time you want. But you will not always have me. She did what she could. She poured perfume on my body beforehand to prepare for my burial. I tell you the truth,**

wherever the gospel is preached throughout the world, what she has done will also be told, in memory of her."

Women should take special note, as this can inspire women's ministries around the globe; it was a female who anointed Jesus. Look at how valuable Jesus' anointing was. The materials used to anoint Jesus were worth **"more than a year's wages."** Jesus calls this anointing **"a beautiful thing."** Jesus wanted people to remember this humble, yet expensive anointing forever, as evident from what he says at the end: **"wherever the gospel is preached throughout the world, what she has done will also be told, in memory of her."** That Jesus wanted people to remember this anointing shows how he felt about the importance of being the Messiah: everyone must know it **"throughout the world."**

On an only somewhat related side note, there are companies even today that sell spikenard mixed with olive oil as a perfume. While it is doubtful that this is what Jesus meant when he prophesied the continual memory of this anointing, it is remarkable to see the impact of this two-thousand year old anointing influence commerce even today.

Let's look at one more definition that needs to become part of our regular vocabulary.

Messianic (adjective). Source: *Oxford Dictionary*

1) Relating to the Messiah: the messianic role of Jesus

2) Inspired by hope or belief in a messiah: the messianic expectations of that time

3) Fervent or passionate: an admirable messianic zeal

It should be noted that the word "messianic" is not in the Bible. However it is still an important term to comprehend. In writing about Christianity, it has become a standard word used to describe things related to Jesus in his role as Messiah.

The purpose of these definitions and this lesson is so that you see a greater need to know the Messiah and are moved to faithful action by the prophecies about the Messiah.

In *The New Evidence that Demands a Verdict*, by Josh McDowell (1999), the author notes that the Old Testament "contains nearly three hundred references to the coming Messiah" (Chapter 8, page 164). Imagine 300 predictions about Jesus' life: all written before the fact and all coming true! That's what you get in the Bible--a lifetime of inspiration.

What follows is a short list of some of the key messianic prophecies that I have found very inspiring and faith-building. Keep in mind that below is not a comprehensive list. Yet just these few are prophecies that can quickly help you to build a great overview. It paints an undeniable picture about who the savior of the world is. This list of prophecies is so rich, that whole sermons and even books could be built around each passage. Some of the verses are covered in greater detail elsewhere in this book, but it's also good to have a quick reference list of powerful prophecies to bookmark. I do encourage you to study them out further on your own.

Short List of Messianic Prophecies Fulfilled

- **David's descendant will be God**: Jeremiah 23:5-6 with Luke 3:23, 31
- **Born of a virgin**: Isaiah 7:14 with Matthew 1:18, 24, 25
- **Born in Bethlehem**: Micah 5:2 with Matthew 2:1
- **Given gifts of gold and frankincense**: Isaiah 60:6 with Matthew 2:11
- **Out of Egypt comes God's son**: Hosea 11:1 with Matthew 2:13-15
- **Ministry begins in Galilee**: Isaiah 9:1 with Matthew 4:12-13, 17
- **Spoke in parables**: Psalm 78:2 with Matthew 13:34-35
- **Undersupply of barley loaves miraculously feeds the multitudes**: 2 Kings 4:42-44 with John 6:8-13
- **Entered Jerusalem on a donkey**: Zechariah 9:9 with Matthew 21:4-7
- **Praised by infants**: Psalm 8:2 with Matthew 21:16
- **Betrayed by a friend**: Psalm 41:9 with Matthew 10:4 and Matthew 26:49-50
- **Sold for 30 silver pieces**: Zechariah 11:12 with Matthew 26:15
- **Wounded and bruised**: Isaiah 53:5 with Matthew 27:26
- **Bones not broken**: Psalm 34:20 with John 19:32-33

- **Pierced (crucified)**: Isaiah 53:5, Zechariah 12:10, Zechariah 13:6 and Psalm 22:16 with Matthew 27:35
  See also Ezra 9:8. In the NIV the term translated as "firm place" is literally a "peg" or "nail."
- **Died with thieves**: Isaiah 53:12 with Matthew 27:38
- **Buried with the rich**: Isaiah 53:9 with Matthew 27:57-60
- **Resurrection**: Psalm 16:10 and Amos 9:11 with Acts 2:31
- **Raised on the 3rd day**: Hosea 6:2 with 1 Corinthians 15:4

After going over these verses in detail, any person in their right mind would have to conclude that Jesus--and only Jesus--fulfills every one of these prophecies to the letter. That's inspiring! Beyond the inspiration, ask yourself how such a list of messianic prophecies might be beneficial to you on a daily basis.

Why Is Messianic Prophecy So Valuable?

1) The overwhelming amount of true predictions about Jesus confirms the accuracy of the Bible and thus increases your faith in God's word.

2) You understand Jesus, your creator and God, thus strengthening your relationship with him.

3) You will read your Bible more, or on a deeper level.

4) You can see the patience and larger plan of God over the centuries.

5) You can help others overcome their doubts about the accuracy of the Bible.

Lists of messianic prophecies always inspire me about the power of God and the perfection of his word. When the church started in Acts 2, one of the characteristics of each member was that **"Everyone was filled with awe..."** (Acts 2:43). The actual Greek word translated as **"awe"** here is "phobos," which means "fear, dread, terror, reverence, and respect." One of the reasons that these disciples were filled with such a powerful emotion is because the Scriptures about the Messiah--God in the flesh--had finally come alive to them as fulfilled prophecies and it rocked their world.

Do you have that same sense of awe about God's word today? In order to grow more in awe of God, my challenge to you is twofold:

1. Add to this list of prophecies as you discover more in God's word.

2. Teach messianic prophecy to others.

In other words, know the Messiah, and make the Messiah known.

It takes patience and faith to step back, as God has, to see the Messiah's comprehensive rescue plan: that's the big picture of salvation. The Scriptures spell this out so prophetically. Along the way, there will be many unforeseen things that may make us trip and stumble in our own boots. I can say this from the bottom of my "sole."

All kidding aside, persevere in God's word and stand on the trustworthy and true prophecies of our Messiah Jesus. Then your footing, like mine, may not always be pretty, but you will be anchored securely on God for an eternity, through a resurrected life.

Chapter 4: Prophecies about the Resurrection

Used 39 times in the New Testament, the Greek word for "resurrection," means "a rising from the dead," according to Thayer's Greek Lexicon. It was a common and controversial topic of discussion in the first century. Frankly, I wish more people were interested in discussions about resurrection today. Almost every writer of the New Testament specifically mentions the resurrection in varying degrees of detail and frequency; this includes all 4 gospel writers as well as Peter, Paul and whomever wrote the book of Hebrews. The only 2 New Testament writers who didn't use the specific term "resurrection" are James and Jude, yet they both strongly imply that there will be a resurrection. Jude states how Jesus will bring the faithful **"to eternal life"** in Jude 1:21, and James 1:12 talks about those who persevere are to **"receive the crown of life."**

Without the resurrection, no one would be interested in the Messiah--at least not for long. But Jesus did rise from the dead, and the predictions about our resurrected Messiah are mounted in the Bible with amazing accuracy long before the actual occurrence.

During the time of the Judges, in 1100 BC, God answered the prayer of a barren woman named Hannah, and she soon gave birth to a son named Samuel. This is a period in history when Israel was not firmly established as a nation, and there was much fighting between them and the Philistines. In Hannah's gratitude over her very young son and future prophet Samuel, she prayed a prayer that contains a most inspiring and prophetic statement. In 1 Samuel 2:6, during the middle of Hannah's prayer, she adds, **"The LORD brings death and makes alive; he brings down to the grave and raises up."**

The way in which Hannah mentions death *before* life is not by accident. Most people, when speaking in general about the life cycle, put life before death, and they certainly don't mention the grave first. A new mother, acting solely by her own thoughts, wouldn't do such a thing. Yet Hannah, because this prayer is specifically about the resurrection, puts life *after* death! It is a prophetic declaration of God allowing Jesus to die, and then raising him up again. We know that the passage is messianic also because the anointed king is also mentioned in 1 Samuel 2:10 as Hannah closes the prayer with **"...He will give strength to his king and exalt the horn of his anointed."** This could also be translated as **"exalt the horn of his Messiah."**

In a broader sense, Hannah putting death before life could additionally be a dual prophecy: describing Jesus' resurrection as well as the resurrection of all the faithful in Christ. What a visionary and blessed woman this was, to be so sure of our resurrection in such a politically unstable time. Hannah should serve as an example of faith to all those who live in uncertain and tumultuous times, waiting long for their prayers to be answered.

Jeremiah 30:8-9 **"'In that day,' declares the LORD Almighty, 'I will break the yoke off their necks and will tear off their bonds; no longer will foreigners enslave them. Instead, they will serve the LORD their God and David their king, whom I will raise up for them.'"**

At the time of Jeremiah's prophecy (600 BC), King David had already been dead for a centuries. Yet Jesus, from the line of David and called **"the son of David"** 16 times in the New Testament, was literally raised up (resurrected) by God. By contrast, after Jesus' resurrection, Peter reminds everyone in Acts 2:29 that King David is still dead. **"Brothers, I can tell you confidently that the patriarch David died and was buried, and his tomb is here to this day."** Clearly then, Jeremiah must be talking about the resurrected Messiah Jesus.

Psalm 16:9-10 **"...my body will also rest secure, because you will not abandon me to the grave, nor will you let your Holy One see decay."**

This is a revolutionary statement; real bodily resurrection was otherwise unheard of, or at least undocumented, when David wrote this around 1,000 BC. Can anyone else say about themselves that they will die, yet their flesh and blood will not decay? The psalmist is saying that Jesus' dead body will rest secure--it won't rot. Think about the last time you were at an open casket funeral or wake. Often when people see a dead body in a funeral home--among the hushed and respectful voices--I've heard mourners whisper how the deceased person "...looks good. Didn't they do a good job with him? He looks so peaceful."

While this may be socially appropriate, is it true? The person they knew isn't even there anymore. What's so painful to accept at that point is that the body has become an empty shell. The dear

27

person's spirit--their life essence--has left the body. If they're so peaceful, and if they look so good, then why are they still dead? The point isn't to belittle those who mourn. Perhaps I too may think similar thoughts the next time I grieve over a loved one. Yet what's so impactful is that Jesus also experienced death yet did not see decay. Beside Enoch and Elijah, who were taken by God in an extraordinary and miraculous manner (Genesis 5:24 and 2 Kings 2:11-12), the rest of the population can't say their bodies won't decay. Other than the resurrected Christ, death and decay are the way of the world.

The Psalm 16:10 prophecy by David is quoted about 1,000 years later by the Apostle Peter in Acts 2:27. After reciting David's prophecy, Peter goes on to explain the passage to be a prophecy specifically about Jesus' resurrection. The body of the Holy One won't **"see decay"** because three days after death, the Christ would rise!

Acts 2:29-32 **"'Brothers, I can tell you confidently that the patriarch David died and was buried, and his tomb is here to this day. But he was a prophet and knew that God had promised him on oath that he would place one of his descendants on his throne. Seeing what was ahead, he spoke of the resurrection of the Christ, that he was not abandoned to the grave, nor did his body see decay. God has raised this Jesus to life, and we are all witnesses of the fact.'"**

Peter said this in front of his contemporaries in Jerusalem who could have easily went to Jesus' burial site to confirm or deny if Jesus' body was there. The location of the tomb was known back then, just as the location of David's tomb was common knowledge. Even the Romans knew the exact spot of Jesus' tomb, since they were the ones who **"made the tomb secure by putting a seal on the stone and posting the guard."** (Matthew 27:66). Yet Jesus was not left by God in the grave because he rose from the dead!

In Psalm 30:3, David prophetically speaks of a resurrected Jesus being brought up from the grave. **"O LORD, you brought me up from the grave; you spared me from going down into the pit."** God is the one who resurrects. He spares from death. The word "grave" used in this verse is the Hebrew word "Sheol." That is by

28

definition, the place of darkness to which all the dead go. In fact, the Gesenius' Hebrew-Chaldee Lexicon states that Sheol is **"a subterranean place, full of thick darkness, in which the shades of the dead are gathered together."** So it's not as if Jesus were buried in a pit or tomb while still alive. The prophecy distinctly says that the person mentioned in Psalm 30:3 is in Sheol! That means the person is dead, yet then brought up by God!

Psalms 41:10 mentioned being raised up as well. **"But you, O LORD, have mercy on me; raise me up, that I may repay them."** The context is not just about the psalmist getting picked up after a fall because the previous verse is a prophecy about Judas' betrayal of Jesus. **"Even my close friend, whom I trusted, he who shared my bread, has lifted up his heel against me."** (Psalms 41:9)

Psalms 118:17 is prophetic of Jesus not staying dead as well. **"I will not die but live, and will proclaim what the LORD has done."** This verse must be about Jesus because a few lines later (Psalm 118:22), Jesus is described just as Peter describes him one thousand years later; **"the stone the builders rejected has become the capstone."** (1 Peter 2:7)

An unforgettable foreshadowing of the resurrection can also be found in Jonah 1:15, 17. **"Then they took Jonah and threw him overboard, and the raging sea grew calm... But the LORD provided a great fish to swallow Jonah, and Jonah was inside the fish three days and three nights."**

Being buried beneath the sea **"three days and three nights"** while inside a great fish is equivalent to the death and burial of Jesus. In Jonah 2:2, this incident is even described as an underground, death-like experience. **"...From the depths of the grave I called for help, and you listened to my cry."**

The great fish submerged deep in the sea is "the grave" for Jonah. God heard Jonah's cry and answered, just as the Father heard Jesus' cry on the cross and answered.

In Jonah 2:4, we even find Jonah prophesying about Jesus resurrection. **"I said, 'I have been banished from your sight; yet I will look again toward your holy temple.'"**

This statement is true for both Jonah and Jesus. Being thrown overboard was Jonah's banishment, while being crucified was Jesus' banishment. Yet neither event was their final fate. Even though it appeared to be final, both Jonah and Jesus, after three days, saw the light of life again.

Jonah 2:6 **"To the roots of the mountains I sank down; the earth beneath barred me in forever. But you brought my life up from the pit, O LORD my God."**

Despite the appearance of being **"barred... in forever,"** both Jonah and Jesus can say that God **"brought my life up from the pit."**

Jesus also confirms that Jonah's experience was a preview of his own death and resurrection in Matthew 12:40. **"For as Jonah was three days and three nights in the belly of a huge fish, so the Son of Man will be three days and three nights in the heart of the earth."**

Jesus refers to this miracle as **"the sign of the prophet Jonah"** (Matthew 12:39). The more you know about the resurrection, the easier it is to connect the dots back to the pioneering prophets who prophesied about it from the days of old. Then these olden days become golden days--rich in truth and ready to be mined for spiritual treasure!

Chapter 5: The Very First Prophecy about Jesus

Starting at the very beginning of the Bible, you don't have to read long at all before you run into the first clear prophecy about Jesus. In fact, look no farther than Genesis 3 in the Garden of Eden. You will find the coming of Jesus, the cross, and his victory over the devil.

After the serpent tricks Adam and Eve into sinning, God delivers the consequences of their sin to them all--not just Adam and Eve's consequences--but also the serpent's consequences. God says something to the serpent that shows God's ultimate rescue plan--right from the beginning.

In Genesis 3:15, describing what will happen in the future, God says to the serpent, **"And I will put enmity between you and the woman, and between your offspring and hers; he will crush your head, and you will strike his heel."**

Let's break this down, because it is a loaded statement. God basically explains that he will put a positive, active hatred (**"enmity"**) between the serpent and the woman, as well as between the serpent's offspring (the devil's followers) and the woman's offspring: Jesus. Within this adversarial relationship, Jesus will **"crush"** the serpent's head, yet first the serpent will strike Jesus' **"heel."**

Galatians 4:4 confirms that Jesus is the offspring of a woman: **"...God sent his Son, born of a woman."** This a true depiction of the virgin birth of Jesus. Biologically speaking, Jesus is not the offspring (seed) of man, but of woman.

Matthew 1:18-20 amazingly sums up who did what as it relates to Mary's pregnancy; **"This is how the birth of Jesus Christ came about: His mother Mary was pledged to be married to Joseph, but before they came together, she was found to be with child through the Holy Spirit. Because Joseph her husband was a righteous man and did not want to expose her to public disgrace, he had in mind to divorce her quietly. But after he had considered this, an angel of the Lord appeared to him in a dream and said, 'Joseph son of David, do not be afraid to take Mary**

home as your wife, because what is conceived in her is from the Holy Spirit.'"

It is interesting to note that the prophecy in Genesis 3:15, combined with Matthew 1, accurately describes Jesus as the offspring of a woman (Mary), yet not the offspring (seed) of a man (Joseph). The very first messianic prophecy in the Bible is well under way. Yet there's more to discover about this passage.

Further examination of the phrase **"you** [the serpent] **will strike his heel"** from Genesis 3:15 is in order. Reading an account of the crucifixion process, it becomes clear that the heel area of the body is severely stricken during the torturous process of nailing a person's feet to a wooden beam and then trying to push yourself up to take a breath. The act of pushing yourself up to breathe while crucified sends burning pain through the nail wounds that shoot relentlessly down the heel. For a most gripping article about this, read "The Medical Account of the Crucifixion of Christ" by Dr. C. Truman Davis.

As if the meaning here in the time of Adam and Eve wasn't already deep enough, there's more to uncover many generations later! From Genesis 25:26, we learn that the name of the patriarch Jacob literally means **"he grabs the heel."** Striking or grabbing the heel is also associated figuratively with deception, and Jacob was known as a deceiver (Genesis 27:36). In the bigger picture of things, Satan is also known as the deceiver. In fact, Revelation 12:9 says that Satan **"leads the whole world astray."** So from the very beginning, the continually deceiving nature of Satan was predicted.

Moreover, since Jacob (a deceiver) is also known by the name "Israel" (Genesis 32:28), this may even predict the deceitful betrayal of God's people (Israel) toward Jesus. After all, it was the Israelites who demanded Jesus' crucifixion before Pontius Pilate.

Matthew 27:22 **"'What shall I do, then, with Jesus who is called Christ?' Pilate asked. They all answered, 'Crucify him!'"**

Clearly, the serpent's deceptive and deadly strike on Jesus was predicted all the way back at the Garden of Eden. That's our mighty God, willing to create and verbalize our rescue plan even from the comfort of paradise. From the security and purity of Garden of Eden-

-a paradise on earth--comes the most bold and bloody plot to save us, despite our often clueless and rebellious nature.

I certainly was clueless and extremely rebellious before I became a disciple of Jesus. Since I was formerly opposed to God, by definition, I was the offspring of the serpent! Yet by the grace of God, he has moved me over to the other side of that adversarial relationship. Now I am the offspring of Eve, the offspring of Jesus, and therefore the enmity is no longer between me and God, but between me and the devil. It's a sobering thought to realize that I was (for too long) operating in opposition to Jesus, and that according to Genesis 3:15, there was enmity (positive, active hatred or ill will) between me and the very person who came up with and carried out the rescue plan.

In his foresight, God planted direction into his Law in so many ways that would culminate at the cross. Jesus, as our Passover sacrifice, hung on the cross, but not overnight. That was no coincidence. It was the plan of God.

Exodus 34:25 **"...do not let any of the sacrifice from the Passover Feast remain until morning."**

Roughly 1400 years before the cross, God sets up rules given to Moses that would make sure that 1400 years later, Jesus would not be left on the cross overnight. This is exactly what happened on that fateful day in Jerusalem to the Lamb of God. John 19:31 confirms this. **"Now it was the day of Preparation, and the next day was to be a special Sabbath. Because the Jews did not want the bodies left on the crosses during the Sabbath, they asked Pilate to have the legs broken and the bodies taken down."** The body of Jesus was taken down the same day in which he was sacrificed, fulfilling the prophetic law in Exodus 34:25. Jesus, the Lamb of God who takes away the sin of the world, did not **"remain until morning."**

The Scriptures make me so much more grateful for second chances and the cross of Christ. Jesus was planning and willing to suffer for us from the very beginning of our history: what a wonderful and loving Messiah and God we have.

Chapter 6: Hanging on a Tree

Outside of the Bible, a Greek historian named Herodotus provides a valuable narrative of crucifixion. Herodotus lived from 484 BC to 425 BC and wrote *The Histories*, which is an account of the Greco-Persian War. Within this work, the ancient historian documents the crucifixion of a Persian general named Artayctes by the Athenians with unnerving similarity to Jesus' later crucifixion.

"...for the people of Elaeus desired that Artayctes should be put to death in revenge for Protesilaus, and the general himself was so inclined. So they carried Artayctes away to the headland where Xerxes had bridged the strait (or, by another story, to the hill above the town of Madytus), and there nailed him to boards and hanged him...." (Herodotus 9.120.4)

Note the similar circumstances between the death of Artayctes and Jesus; the people desire the person to die, the condemned man is a leader, he's led away from the city to a hill in view of the city, he's nailed to wood, and he is hung up on public display until death. The two deaths are about 500 years apart, yet the many similarities point to a common cultural practice that was repeated as the people deemed necessary in ancient times.

Perhaps using Herodotus as one of his sources, it had been researched by Dr. C. Truman Davis (a graduate of the University of Tennessee College of Medicine), that **"Apparently, the first known practice of crucifixion was by the Persians. Alexander and his generals brought it back to the Mediterranean world--to Egypt and to Carthage. The Romans apparently learned the practice from the Carthaginians..."** Dr. Davis originally said this in an article called *The Medical Account of the Crucifixion of Christ*. It was first published in Arizona Medicine, March 1965, by Arizona Medical Association.

For over 16 years I have highly regarded Dr. Davis' research, and still do so. I have referred many people to this amazing article, as it does give the modern reader a more comprehensive view of what exactly happened to Jesus on the cross. Nevertheless, deeper research into the Scriptures has led me to understand that crucifixion may have evolved from even earlier times than the Persians. I'm not saying that crucifixion was, or wasn't occurring before the Persians. Yet the practice of hanging a person from a tree as a form of public capital punishment is a much earlier practice. I cite the following verses as examples.

In Genesis 40:19, while in jail, Joseph interpreted the chief baker's dream by saying, **"Within three days Pharaoh will lift off your head and hang you on a tree. And the birds will eat away your flesh."** Three days later, the chief baker was indeed hanged (Genesis 40:22). It might be assumed here that this hanging was done with ropes, but we really don't know how it was done: ropes, nails, clamps, who knows? In fact, the word **"hanged"** in verse 22 is also translated as "impaled." The year was about 1890 BC, well over one thousand years before the Persian Empire.

The following verse is a key Scripture. It's a 1400 BC law and also a prophetic description of Jesus on the cross.

Deuteronomy 21:22-23 **"If a man guilty of a capital offense is put to death and his body is hung on a tree, you must not leave his body on the tree overnight. Be sure to bury him that same day, because anyone who is hung on a tree is under God's curse. You must not desecrate the land the LORD your God is giving you as an inheritance."**

What leaves me staggering about the above verse is that God designed a law that would painfully influence his own crucifixion and prophetically detail how Jesus would become a "curse" for us by taking on our guilt. This is confirmed in Galatians 3:13. **"Christ redeemed us from the curse of the law by becoming a curse for us, for it is written: 'Cursed is everyone who is hung on a tree.'"** If you combine Deuteronomy 21 with its descriptive fulfillment in Galatians 3, it becomes unnervingly clear that God had crucifixion specifically in mind when he wrote this law to Moses around 1400 BC.

Let this sink into our heads; Jesus was **"cursed"** at the cross and this was no random, last minute sequence of unfortunate events. It was the very plan of God from ancient times. To be cursed is from a root word that means "to be despised, to treat with contempt" (Gesenius' Hebrew-Chaldee Lexicon). Looking at the Merriam-Webster definition, a curse is a prayer or invocation for harm or injury to come upon someone. It's evil or misfortune that comes as retribution. A curse is a cause of great harm or misfortune.

Every aspect of this definition precisely describes what happens when someone is hung on a tree--including Jesus. For the guilty, to be cursed might seem like a fitting response to some terrible crime. Yet for the innocent to be cursed, a spirit of injustice and alarm is invoked. Understand on a heart-level that Jesus was completely innocent, yet hung on a tree for our sin. The curse should have fallen upon us: the sinners. Instead it fell hard and heavy, on Jesus.

Continuing our study of cases where people are hung on a tree, Joshua 8:29 shows that the practice was used, not just by God's enemies, but also by God's followers. During 1406 BC, Joshua, while taking the Promised Land did this; **"He hung the king of Ai on a tree and left him there until evening. At sunset, Joshua ordered them to take his body from the tree and throw it down at the entrance of the city gate. And they raised a large pile of rocks over it, which remains to this day**." Notice also that, as an obedient leader, Joshua follows God's command from Deuteronomy 21:22 about not letting the body hang overnight. Also obedient, the Jews did the same with Jesus' body over 1400 years later. **"Now it was the day of Preparation, and the next day was to be a special Sabbath. Because the Jews did not want the bodies left on the crosses during the Sabbath, they asked Pilate to have the legs broken and the bodies taken down."** (John 19:31). It's ironic that all of us, as a society, can follow some laws without fail for generation after generation, yet miss the heart behind God's fundamental law to love one another.

It is unnerving to realize that the king of Ai, the Egyptian chief baker, and innocent King Jesus shared in a similar punishment: being hung on a tree. As is the case with the Egyptian chief baker, we don't know how the hanging of the king of Ai was done: whether ropes, nails, or some other practice was used to hang the person on a tree.

Around 520 BC, the Bible confirms the Persian use of punishment by hanging on a tree in a number of places. Most notably, in Ezra 6:11, King Darius punctuates a certain law with this warning; **"Furthermore, I decree that if anyone changes this**

edict, a beam is to be pulled from his house and he is to be lifted up and impaled on it. And for this crime his house is to be made a pile of rubble." This Persian king's regulation gives evidence that being hung on a tree by impaling was an existing form of punishment, unless the king, heated with indignation, just invented the practice to scare the masses. Here it sounds most specifically like this is a form of crucifixion. In fact, according to Gesenius' Hebrew-Chaldee Lexicon, the word translated in Ezra 6:11 as "impaled" literally means "to crucify" in the Syriac language (also known as Syriac Aramaic).

Another significant biblical hanging on a tree during the Persian Empire is the 75 feet high hanging of Haman, the treacherous advisor to the king around 470 BC. Haman's punishment was originally intended for Mordecai (Esther 5:14), but God delivered Mordecai and showed him to the king as a man of integrity. **"So they hanged Haman on the gallows he had prepared for Mordecai. Then the king's fury subsided"** (Esther 7:10).

Hanging from a tree as a form of the most severe punishment has a long and dark history. With Jesus being all-knowing, it makes me wonder what Jesus might have been thinking each time a person was hung on a tree throughout the ages.

Chapter 7: Supernatural Lineage

God had his mighty hand in crafting the lineage of the Messiah throughout the generations leading up to the birth of Jesus in Roman times. This fact is well documented and quite inspirational. To fully appreciate this grand design of God, here is a much abbreviated view of Jesus' family tree:

Luke 3:23, 31, 33, 34, 36, 38 **"Now Jesus himself was about thirty years old when he began his ministry. He was the son, so it was thought, of Joseph... the son of David... the son of Judah, the son of Jacob, the son of Isaac, the son of Abraham... the son of Shem, the son of Noah... the son of Enosh, the son of Seth, the son of Adam, the son of God."**

Studying these ancestors can give you great insight into the coming of Jesus Christ. Let's look at some key points and prophecies in this lineage of Jesus.

From the Line of Abram/Abraham

Genesis 12:1-3 **"The LORD had said to Abram, 'Leave your country, your people and your father's household and go to the land I will show you. I will make you into a great nation and I will bless you; I will make your name great, and you will be a blessing. I will bless those who bless you, and whoever curses you I will curse; and all peoples on earth will be blessed through you.'"**

God promised to make Abram (later renamed Abraham) **"into a great nation... and all peoples on earth will be blessed through"** Abram. God actually makes this promise to Abraham at least two more times in Genesis (18:18 and 22:18). This great promise is also regarded as the announcement of the gospel in advance, as confirmed by Paul in Galatians.

Galatians 3:8 **"The Scripture foresaw that God would justify the Gentiles by faith, and announced the gospel in advance to Abraham: 'All nations will be blessed through you.'"**

The followers of Jesus are blessed from all nations because of the great sacrifice and love shown by Jesus at the cross. From ancient times, God called Abraham by faith and he is calling you today!

From the Line of Isaac

Speaking to Abraham about his son Isaac, God says that an everlasting covenant will be established through Isaac.

Genesis 17:19 **"Then God said, 'Yes, but your wife Sarah will bear you a son, and you will call him Isaac. I will establish my covenant with him as an everlasting covenant for his descendants after him.'"**

This everlasting covenant is a reference to Jesus' new covenant in his blood--through the cross.

From the Line of Jacob

God continues to reconfirm his promise to bless all peoples through Abraham by repeating the promise to Abraham's grandson Jacob in one of the most amazing dreams of all time.

Genesis 28:10-19 **"Jacob left Beersheba and set out for Haran. When he reached a certain place, he stopped for the night because the sun had set. Taking one of the stones there, he put it under his head and lay down to sleep. He had a dream in which he saw a stairway resting on the earth, with its top reaching to heaven, and the angels of God were ascending and descending on it. There above it stood the LORD, and he said: 'I am the LORD, the God of your father Abraham and the God of Isaac. I will give you and your descendants the land on which you are lying. Your descendants will be like the dust of the earth, and you will spread out to the west and to the east, to the north and to the south. All peoples on earth will be blessed through you and your offspring. I am with you and will watch over you wherever you go, and I will bring you back to this land. I will not leave you until I have done what I have promised you.' When Jacob awoke from his sleep, he thought, 'Surely the LORD is in this place, and I was not aware of it.' He was afraid and said, 'How awesome is this place! This is none other than the house of God; this is the gate of heaven.' Early the next morning Jacob took the stone he had placed under his head and set it up as a pillar and poured oil on top of it. He called that place Bethel, though the city used to be called Luz."**

The name of the place where Jacob had this dream is called Bethel, which means "house of God." As with Abraham, we are blessed through Jacob's offspring Jesus, who is the cornerstone of the house of God (Ephesians 2:20).

Jacob is shown the stairway to heaven, and he describes this place as **"the gate of heaven."** Imagine that: seeing a structure that goes from the ground in front of you all the way up to as far as your eyes can see upwards into the sky. God is helping us to see that it is through the lineage of his people--which culminates in Jesus Christ-- that we too can have access to inconceivable heights, even to the gate of heaven. Not coincidentally, Jesus also describes himself as **"the gate"** twice in John 10.

John 10:7, 9 **"...I tell you the truth, I am the gate for the sheep.... I am the gate; whoever enters through me will be saved."**

We see that going through Jesus is a salvation issue. He is the way to heaven and we must go through him.

Getting back to Genesis 28, after his dream of the stairway to heaven, Jacob makes an observation that we would do well to respect and learn from even today. He came to understand that the LORD was in that place, but he **"was not aware of it."** How often do we go about our business with no regard for where God is or what he might be doing? We need to be more aware of God's promises and his presence in our lives.

From the Line of Judah

The patriarch Jacob, when he was about to die, gathered his 12 sons together to bless them and to tell them **"what will happen to you in days to come"** (Genesis 49:1). Reading through all of his son's blessings, it is clear that they mostly refer to predictions pertaining to Jacob's actual sons present at the hearing of this blessing as well as events that will happen in the coming generations. However, what Jacob says about his son Judah is unique, to say the least.

Genesis 49:8-10 **"Judah, your brothers will praise you; your hand will be on the neck of your enemies; your father's sons will bow down to you. You are a lion's cub, O Judah; you return**

40

from the prey, my son. Like a lion he crouches and lies down, like a lioness--who dares to rouse him? The scepter will not depart from Judah, nor the ruler's staff from between his feet, until he comes to whom it belongs and the obedience of the nations is his."

Of all the brothers, only Judah (or as we understand it, a descendant of Judah) will receive praise from his brothers and they "will bow down to" him. Jacob also says that "The scepter will not depart from Judah...." This shows that a lineage of kings will come from Judah.

It is well known that none of these prophecies came true of Jacob's actual son Judah. He wasn't a king, and his brothers never bowed down to him. So this is all about Jesus. Continuing to speak about the lineage of Judah, Jacob elaborates with details that easily link to Jesus:

Genesis 49:11-12 "He will tether his donkey to a vine, his colt to the choicest branch; he will wash his garments in wine, his robes in the blood of grapes. His eyes will be darker than wine, his teeth whiter than milk."

These statements are allusions to Jesus. After all, the week prior to being crucified, Jesus rode into Jerusalem on a donkey (Matthew 21:7), and he even calls himself "the true vine" (John 15:1). Also, right before being crucified, he was flogged and then a scarlet robe was put on him with a crown of thorns (Matthew 27:26-29). Metaphorically speaking, that's how Jesus washed "his garments in wine, his robes in the blood of grapes." It's a prophecy leading up to the cross.

From the Line of David

The following heart-warming and soul-stirring prophecy mentions David, but it takes place centuries after David's death, so it has to be about Jesus, the good shepherd.

Ezekiel 37:24-28 "My servant David will be king over them, and they will all have one shepherd. They will follow my laws and be careful to keep my decrees. They will live in the land I gave to my servant Jacob, the land where your fathers lived. They and their children and their children's children will live

41

there forever, and David my servant will be their prince forever. I will make a covenant of peace with them; it will be an everlasting covenant. I will establish them and increase their numbers, and I will put my sanctuary among them forever. My dwelling place will be with them; I will be their God, and they will be my people. Then the nations will know that I the LORD make Israel holy, when my sanctuary is among them forever."

God's servant "David" will be their **"prince forever"**! Since David has long been passed away at the time Ezekiel spoke this, the statement has to be regarded as a messianic prophecy. It's an encouraging reference to the eternal kingdom of the **"one shepherd,"** Jesus Christ, descended from the line of David. Since God will **"increase their numbers,"** and put his **"sanctuary among them forever,"** this must be a prophecy about the numerical growth of the church. Let that be a word of caution for all: if your church isn't increasing with new faithful members who **"are careful to keep** [God's] **decrees,"** then you have to ask yourself, "Am I really part of Jesus' church?"

God's **"dwelling place will be with"** the people in **"a covenant of peace"** forever through Jesus' Holy Spirit. Members of the true church can have peace with God and peace with each other: no more unrest, no more fighting. Again, if you don't have peace with God and the members of the church, something is amiss. It is up to you to figure out in your life and doctrine what exactly went wrong.

For about three agonizing years, my wife and I were part of a church who had stopped growing and quite suddenly had no peace. After much prayer, Bible study, and advice, we finally realized that the entire group--us included--were in all kinds of sin. Therefore, my wife and I repented, called the church to repent, and regrouped/reformed with disciples who still wanted to hold to God's standard over the status quo traditions of mankind. Almost immediately, this new group started rapidly growing in numbers, in peace with God, and in peace with each other. Isn't that awesome? When appropriately applied to our lives, the ancient prophecies about the Messiah can set us on a right path--right way.

What is even more exciting is that this verse from Ezekiel 37:24-28 reminds us that these earthly challenges will not last very long compared to eternity. With the 5 references to **"forever"** and **"everlasting,"** we are also assured that the faithful members of the church will continue dwelling with God after death in paradise for all eternity. Don't you want to go to that land?

Chapter 8: God Has a Son, and That's a Big Deal

Fathers and sons are a core concept of humanity. In fact, the father-son relationship has been designed by God as one of the main ways in which we are supposed to learn about the nature of our Father in heaven.

Proverbs 2:1-5 **"My son, if you accept my words and store up my commands within you, turning your ear to wisdom and applying your heart to understanding, and if you call out for insight and cry aloud for understanding, and if you look for it as for silver and search for it as for hidden treasure, then you will understand the fear of the LORD and find the knowledge of God."**

The godly pattern is quite simple: the father teaches his son godly commands and the result is that the son who applies these commands with all intensity will know God as a direct result. The purpose of having a son is to transfer knowledge of God down the family line. This can best be seen in God the Father's relationship with Jesus his son.

Reading the Bible, it is obvious that Jesus is described, not just as a son, but as the son of God. How is that significant? Is this a new concept: that Jesus is a son? Not at all. Most casual readers of the Bible miss this fact, yet this son of God was active long before being born in a manger at Bethlehem (Luke 2:4-7). Cruising through the Old Testament, this son of God is actually all over the place. Here are a few key Scriptures that display the presence and great importance of the son of God.

Genesis 1:26-27 **"Then God said, 'Let us make man in our image, in our likeness....' So God created man in his own image, in the image of God he created him; male and female he created them."**

Right from the beginning we are told that there are at least two mighty agents crucially involved in the creation of our world and our ancestors. God refers to himself with plural statements such as **"Let us"** and **"our image, our likeness."** So who is God talking to here? Look at John 1:1-4, which describes the Word as being **"with God"** and also that **"the Word was God,"** as the creator. We see further in John 1:14 that **"The Word became flesh and made his dwelling among us...."** This Word who became flesh is Jesus. Therefore back in Genesis, either God the Father is talking or God the Son is talking, or both. That's a big deal because it shows, not only how much more active the son has been in our entire history, but also it shows Jesus to be God.

What is even more remarkable from Genesis 1:26 is God's statement to **"make man in our image, in our likeness."** The Father and Son have an image and a likeness that they decide to replicate in man. So Father and Son look alike, because we are made in their image and likeness. Consider this the next time you are tempted to look at another human being with hatred; you are hating the image and likeness of God the Father and Jesus the Son.

Further evidence of this Father/Son/God relationship can be seen in Genesis 3:22. Who is God talking to after Adam and Eve ate the forbidden fruit? **"And the LORD God said, 'The man has now become like one of us, knowing good and evil."** Note how God says that man has **"become like one of us."** The **"us"** must be Father and Son.

In Psalm 2:6-7, the LORD gets right to the point about the one whom he has installed as king in Zion. **"I have installed my king on Zion, my holy hill. I will proclaim the decree of the LORD: He said to me, 'You are my Son; today I have become your**

Father.'" See the significance of the relationship; God wants everyone to know that he has a king who is his son to be followed and adored. The LORD wraps up this statement by commanding to **"Kiss the Son, lest he be angry and you be destroyed on your way, for his wrath can flair up in a moment. Blessed are all who take refuge in him"** (Psalm 2:12). Note who is blessed: those who take security in Jesus the Son.

Proverbs 30:4 also talks about the amazing creator and his son. **"Who has gone up to heaven and come down? Who has gathered up the wind in the hollow of his hands? Who has wrapped up the waters in his cloak? Who has established all the ends of the earth? What is his name, and the name of his son? Tell me if you know!"**

The same nature-commanding being who **"has gone up to heaven and come down"** and who **"has established the ends of the earth"** has a son, so he must be a father.

Written around 700 AD, in Hosea 11:1, God says **"When Israel was a child, I loved him, and out of Egypt I called my son."** Reading the rest of the chapter, the context seems to be about the people of Israel. However, seven centuries later, this **"out of Egypt"** statement is confirmed by Matthew to be a prophecy specifically about Jesus.

Matthew 2:13-15 **"When they had gone, an angel of the Lord appeared to Joseph in a dream. 'Get up,' he said, 'take the child and his mother and escape to Egypt. Stay there until I tell you, for Herod is going to search for the child to kill him.' So he got up, took the child and his mother during the night and left for Egypt, where he stayed until the death of Herod. And so was fulfilled what the Lord had said through the prophet: 'Out of Egypt I called my son.'"**

What is so remarkable about this prophecy is that God loves his son and even has his son go through an Egyptian period of refuge, just like the twelve tribes did in the days of Jacob and Joseph. Despite the bad times, God always has a plan. Often there is a grand symmetry to God's plan that seems to be there simply to inspire us to connect the dots back to the Messiah--back to Jesus. I so appreciate God's design for our lives.

Written roughly during the same period as Hosea, in Isaiah 7:14, the son is prophesied about as being Immanuel, which means **"God with us."** We see also that this is given by God through a virgin birth. **"Therefore the Lord himself will give you a sign: The virgin will be with child and will give birth to a son, and will call him Immanuel."**

This child Immanuel didn't fade into ancient obscurity. By Isaiah 8:7-10, Immanuel is associated with the lands of Judah. **"Therefore the Lord is about to bring against them the mighty floodwaters of the River--the king of Assyria with all his pomp. It will overflow all its channels, run over all its banks and sweep on into Judah, swirling over it, passing through it and reaching up to the neck. Its outspread wings will cover the breadth of your land, O Immanuel! Raise the war cry, you nations, and be shattered! Listen, all you distant lands. Prepare for battle, and be shattered! Prepare for battle, and be shattered! Devise your strategy, but it will be thwarted; propose your plan, but it will not stand, for God is with us."**

What is so encouraging about this messianic passage is that things get bad, yet God comes through with a victory in the end: **"propose your plan, but it will not stand, for God is with us."** Another way to translate that last part is **"propose your plan, but it will not stand because of Immanuel."**

Clearly, the child Immanuel (God with us) grows into a great leader and rescuer, despite overwhelming conflict. That is the predicted role of the Messiah and the fulfilled mission of Jesus.

The Son of God Is God the Father

Continuing through Isaiah 9:1-7, in no uncertain terms, the Scriptures declare the fullness of who this remarkable child is.

1 "Nevertheless, there will be no more gloom for those who were in distress. In the past he humbled the land of Zebulun and the land of Naphtali, but in the future he will honor Galilee of the Gentiles, by the way of the sea, along the Jordan--

2 The people walking in darkness have seen a great light; on those living in the land of the shadow of death a light has dawned.

3 **You have enlarged the nation and increased their joy; they rejoice before you as people rejoice at the harvest, as men rejoice when dividing the plunder.**

4 **For as in the day of Midian's defeat, you have shattered the yoke that burdens them, the bar across their shoulders, the rod of their oppressor.**

5 **Every warrior's boot used in battle and every garment rolled in blood will be destined for burning, will be fuel for the fire.**

6 **For to us a child is born, to us a son is given, and the government will be on his shoulders. And he will be called Wonderful Counselor, Mighty God, Everlasting Father, Prince of Peace.**

7 **Of the increase of his government and peace there will be no end. He will reign on David's throne and over his kingdom, establishing and upholding it with justice and righteousness from that time on and forever. The zeal of the LORD Almighty will accomplish this."**

This passage is a wealth of bold and true statements about Jesus. A simple rephrasing of these verses explain the following: Light and freedom will come to the people through Galilee by way of a son born as a descendant of King David. This son will be an everlasting king in an everlasting kingdom. He is the amazing Counselor, God the Father and the Prince of Peace. These three attributes accurately detail the trinity concept. Jesus, as Holy Spirit (**"Wonderful Counselor"**), Father (**"Mighty God, Everlasting Father"**), and Son (**"Prince of Peace"**) operates as three manifestations of God. Put simply, whether active as an invisible deity or in the form of a tangible being, Jesus, the Son of God, is God the Father.

Isaiah 9:7 solidifies this reality in stone by giving us a God-backed guarantee that the events described will definitely happen. In no uncertain terms, Isaiah says, **"The zeal of the LORD Almighty will accomplish this."** In other words, Jesus is God and savior, and that is a done-deal. Nothing will stop this rescue plan from succeeding.

That is why, in Isaiah 9:1, it says that **"there will be no more gloom for those who were in distress."** The over-the top

48

confidence and reliability of the Scriptures counsel me with great comfort that the Father, Son, and Holy Spirit, unified as one **"Mighty God,"** will take care of me as I lay my burdens down. So no more gloom for you, and no more gloom for me.

In Isaiah 49:5-6, we see another important reason why Jesus is known as God's son. **"And now the LORD says-- he who formed me in the womb to be his servant to bring Jacob back to him and gather Israel to himself, for I am honored in the eyes of the LORD and my God has been my strength--he says: 'It is too small a thing for you to be my servant to restore the tribes of Jacob and bring back those of Israel I have kept. I will also make you a light for the Gentiles, that you may bring my salvation to the ends of the earth.'"**

From these verses we learn that God's son will become a real man **"formed"** by God **"in the womb."** This God-honored servant will "restore the tribes of Jacob" and be made **"a light to the Gentiles."** That, of course, is Jesus, who brings God's **"salvation to the ends of the earth."** We are assured by God that he will send his son as a savior on a global scale. All nations can benefit from his light.

As part of the same discourse in Isaiah 49:7-8, God reveals more details about his son that can only refer to specific facts about Jesus' life. **"This is what the LORD says--the Redeemer and Holy One of Israel--to him who was despised and abhorred by the nation, to the servant of rulers: 'Kings will see you and rise up, princes will see and bow down, because of the LORD, who is faithful, the Holy One of Israel, who has chosen you.' This is what the LORD says: 'In the time of my favor I will answer you, and in the day of salvation I will help you; I will keep you and will make you to be a covenant for the people, to restore the land and to reassign its desolate inheritances,'"**

God's son was **"despised and abhorred by the nation,"** yet **"princes will see and bow down."** Moreover, God makes his son **"to be a covenant for the people."** Who else could this be describing? Jesus was despised at the cross by his own nation, yet made **"to be a covenant for the people."**

How was Jesus made into a covenant? See 1 Corinthians 11:25. **"In the same way, after supper he took the cup, saying, 'This cup is the new covenant in my blood; do this, whenever you drink it, in remembrance of me.'"** Jesus explains that the new covenant is within his own blood. Again we are taken back to the cross, where his blood was shed for our sake.

Father and Son Questions: Answering the Skeptics

There are those who try to limit God's ability by posing the question, "How can God be both the Father and the Son? Isn't that a contradiction?" I've had Muslims in Chicago pose this question as a sorry attempt to discredit Christianity. Yet the real question to think about, if you respect God's unlimited power, is this; "Since God can do whatever he wants, why couldn't he be both Father and Son?" Just because we can't fathom being both father and son, it doesn't mean that Jesus is barred from being who he is: Father and Son.

Oh, wait. There's a relatable parallel in there. Perhaps you picked up on it. Indeed, we can be both father and son. I am a father to my three children, yet I'm also a son to my Dad who raised me. Along with the majority of the male population, I am father and son. I operate as such on a human scale. God operates as such on a supernatural scale.

Jesus is also described as a son (and more) in Daniel 7:13-14. **"In my vision at night I looked, and there before me was one like a son of man, coming with the clouds of heaven. He approached the Ancient of Days and was led into his presence. He was given authority, glory and sovereign power; all peoples, nations and men of every language worshiped him. His dominion is an everlasting dominion that will not pass away, and his kingdom is one that will never be destroyed."**

Take note of the power that this **"son of man"** has. He comes **"with the clouds of heaven."** He's in the presence of God, **"the Ancient of Days."** This son is given **"sovereign power"** and everyone in every place **"worshiped him."** To top it off, his dominion is **"everlasting"** and his kingdom **"will never be destroyed."**

Jesus is the only son who fits such a description, and he's the only son whom we must worship. Of course if everyone is to worship him, then he must be God, because 2 Kings 17:38-39 reiterates how worshiping other gods is forbidden. **"Do not forget the covenant I have made with you, and do not worship other gods. Rather, worship the LORD your God; it is he who will deliver you from the hand of all your enemies."**

Therefore we are left with the only logical conclusion a person can make. Worship this son of man because he is the king of the everlasting kingdom. This makes perfect sense, because Jesus is God.

Chapter 9: The Anointed One Is Set Above

Let's try a messianic exercise. What is the most impressive thing anyone has ever said about you? Perhaps it might be one of these encouraging phrases.

"You're awesome!"

"You're so faithful!"

"You're so talented!"

"You're so amazing!"

Have any of these statements ever applied to you? Are any still true about you today? If you are like most people, you may have your moments of inspiration, but at the end of the day, you are still a sinner--like us all. Now let's look at a person that someone said some very remarkable things about in the Bible--and they're all true.

Psalm 45 **"For the director of music. To the tune of 'Lilies.' Of the Sons of Korah. A maskil. A wedding song.**

1 My heart is stirred by a noble theme as I recite my verses for the king; my tongue is the pen of a skillful writer.

2 You are the most excellent of men and your lips have been anointed with grace, since God has blessed you forever.

3 Gird your sword upon your side, O mighty one; clothe yourself with splendor and majesty.

4 In your majesty ride forth victoriously in behalf of truth, humility and righteousness; let your right hand display awesome deeds.

5 Let your sharp arrows pierce the hearts of the king's enemies; let the nations fall beneath your feet.

6 Your throne, O God, will last for ever and ever; a scepter of justice will be the scepter of your kingdom.

7 You love righteousness and hate wickedness; therefore God, your God, has set you above your companions by anointing you with the oil of joy."

These are more than just impressive statements and fluffy poetry. Our hearts need to be **"stirred"** up (verse 1) **"by a noble theme"** for our King Jesus. Indeed, I am so grateful to be part of a church wherein the members are excited to worship and live out the gospel in an everyday manner. The noble theme is Jesus' heart to have a relationship with us, save us by his grace, and take his noble theme to all nations.

Now take a moment to compare what is said about this king to what people say about you. Speaking from a pure-hearted perspective, has anyone told you that **"your lips have been anointed with grace"**? No? Me neither. Chalk it up as one more reason to stand in awe of God and imitate Jesus, who has been anointed with grace as **"the most excellent of men."**

No one compares to Jesus; no one is more excellent than he. Does your life reflect this? When you look at your own role models, is Jesus at the forefront? He needs to be. In fact, people should be able to look at your life and see characteristics of Jesus in you. That's the whole point of why he said over and over to **"follow me."** That command is used by Jesus 20 times in the New Testament (Matthew 4:19, etc.).

In the Old Testament, when the Israelites would talk about the anointed one--the Messiah--there was heightened interest and great expectations. Looking for **"the most excellent of men,"** they expected their Messiah, as king, to come and deliver them into great victories. The Israelites were really worked up about the Messiah. How about you? Are you worked up about the Messiah?

Take a closer look at Psalm 45. Who is the psalmist speaking about in verse 7? "**...therefore God, your God, has set you above your companions by anointing you with the oil of joy."** How many individuals are being addressed as God here? The person being talked about in this passage goes from being a king blessed by God forever (verse 1 and 2) to having an eternal kingdom (verse 6) to being the anointed God set above his companions (verse 7) by God.

These are true statements about Jesus who is identified as none other than God himself. At the very least, the concept of God addressing someone as "God" who has been set **"above"** his companions might be puzzling to the first hearers of this. But Jesus fulfills this prophecy exactly. Carefully rereading verse 7 shows that Jesus, the Messiah is addressed as "God," and while this Messiah is addressed as God, this same Messiah/God also has his own God (as in God the Father) who has set the Messiah above his companions.

Psalm 45 is mighty with messianic meaning. It is quoted about one thousand years later in Hebrews 1:8-9. **"But about the Son he says, 'Your throne, O God, will last for ever and ever, and righteousness will be the scepter of your kingdom. You have loved righteousness and hated wickedness; therefore God, your God, has set you above your companions by anointing you with the oil of joy.'"**

The whole passage is **"about the Son."** That's Jesus. But who is the speaker who says **"Your throne, O God..."**? Who is addressing Jesus as God? To understand this, we simply need to look more carefully at what was said just prior to this. Here is a verse by verse outline of Hebrews 1:1-9

1 **"In the past God spoke to our forefathers through the prophets at many times and in various ways,**

2 **but in these last days he has spoken to us by his Son, whom he appointed heir of all things, and through whom he made the universe.**

3 **The Son is the radiance of God's glory and the exact representation of his being, sustaining all things by his powerful word. After he had provided purification for sins, he sat down at the right hand of the Majesty in heaven.**

4 **So he became as much superior to the angels as the name he has inherited is superior to theirs.**

5 **For to which of the angels did God ever say, 'You are my Son; today I have become your Father'? Or again, 'I will be his Father, and he will be my Son'?**

6 **And again, when God brings his firstborn into the world, he says, 'Let all God's angels worship him.'**

7 **In speaking of the angels he says, 'He makes his angels winds, his servants flames of fire.'**

8 **But about the Son he says, 'Your throne, O God, will last for ever and ever, and righteousness will be the scepter of your kingdom.**

9 **You have loved righteousness and hated wickedness; therefore God, your God, has set you above your companions by anointing you with the oil of joy.'"**

From these verses we can see the following.

- God the Father is speaking **"in these last days"** through his Son, Jesus (verse 1 and 2).
- God **"made the universe"** through his Son (verse 2), so this is no ordinary son. This son was with God in the very beginning of creation.
- Jesus, who has **"provided purification for sins,"** is **"the exact representation"** of God (verse 3). Here we have a powerfully direct biblical statement that Jesus is **"the exact representation of"** God: not similar but **"exact."** That can only mean that Jesus is God.
- Jesus' powerful word is **"sustaining all things"** (verse 3). Who else but God can speak things into existence and sustainability simply by the meaningful words he has spoken?
- Jesus is **"superior to the angels"** (verse 4). Of course he is, because he's God.
- From verses 5 through 9, God the Father speaks specifically about God the Son. God, who is described as the Father (verse 5) describes God the Son as he who is worshipped by angels (verse 6), and as God everlasting with a throne, with a righteous kingdom (verse 8), and set above with the anointing oil of joy (verse 9)!

These two passages, Psalm 45 with Hebrews 1, provide a great way to help people who have been deceived by the false teaching that "The Bible never says Jesus is God," or "Jesus never claimed to be God." Nothing could be further from the truth! In fact, Hebrews 1 is one of my favorite passages to help people wondering "Where in the Bible does it say that Jesus is God?" Clearly, the Scriptures identify Jesus as being God, with an everlasting kingdom, and above all.

As if that were not enough, see Hebrews 1:10. **"He also says, 'In the beginning, O Lord, you laid the foundations of the earth, and the heavens are the work of your hands.'"**

Here, God the Father addresses Jesus as **"Lord."** That's because the Father and Son are unified--they are one. Therefore, do you respect Jesus as being your God and your Lord above all? If so, that would mean you obey him as your master. We all need to ask ourselves the following question every day; "Am I doing what the anointed one says?

Looking back at Psalm 45:7, do you understand and appreciate that Jesus--as God--is anointed **"with the oil of joy"**? Jesus is joyful. This is the God we worship: one covered in joy. Therefore, on a personal level, how about you? Are you known for your joy in connection with God? Do you **"laugh at the days to come,"** as characterized by the faithful woman from Psalm 31:25? If not, then why not? What, or who, is blocking your joy?

Often the answer to the above question is our own selves. Therefore, if your joy level is usually low, or if it mostly comes from other sources, then you lack understanding about the anointed one of God, the Messiah, the Christ, God in the flesh, namely Jesus. Don't merely pretend to be joyful. Repent of whatever is holding you back. Trust God on a deeper level to find the joy he is calling you to embrace.

My challenge--for us all--is to really get to know the Messiah. Then and only then will you have access to true joy that lasts forever in his righteous kingdom.

Chapter 10: Statements, Dreams, Visions and Events

There is so much depth to messianic prophecy that I am convinced that a person can spend the rest of their life studying this topic yet never run out of new discoveries or insights into our mighty God. One useful concept about prophecy is to understand that prophecy comes in different forms, and each form holds vital clues into who God is and why the Scriptures are vital to our lives today.

Forms of Prophecy

There are generally four ways, or forms, in which God introduces prophecy to man: statements, dreams, visions and events. God uses all of these methods in the Bible, sometimes in combination, and sometimes by themselves. I will outline these four types of prophecy, beginning with the most common type: statements. This is the type that all other prophecies get oiled down into, namely prophetic statements written down in the Bible.

1. Statements

Prophecy is told using statements that are often puzzling and even riddle-like at the time of their saying. In a prophetic statement, the message is spoken and written down, such as in Micah 5:2 where the birthplace of the Messiah is predicted 500 years before the fact. **"But you, Bethlehem Ephrathah, though you are small among the clans of Judah, out of you will come for me one who will be ruler over Israel, whose origins are from of old, from ancient times."**

Micah uses descriptive statements here to present a scenario that seems a bit like a riddle: **"a ruler over Israel"** will come at a later date, **"whose origins are from old, from ancient times."** In other words, the Messiah will be born in the future, yet he already exists-- even from ancient times. Of course this statement makes no sense except when applied to Jesus, and then it makes perfect, prophetic sense.

This is the most common way that prophecy is transmitted: from statements in sentences that were designed to be put together as part of a larger prophetic puzzle. In the case of Micah 5:2, the statement is so prophetically clear that even the evil King Herod perceives this as a threat to his own power in Matthew 2. In about 3 BC, Herod understands that the Messiah will come from the tribe of Judah, and be born in Bethlehem. So certain is King Herod of this prophecy that he orders the killing of all babies born in Bethlehem at that time. Now if someone so opposed to God can generate such evil due to messianic prophecy, how much more so should we be stirred to godly action and good deeds by messianic prophecy?

So much more can be said about this first type of prophecy: statement based prophecy, since there are hundreds of statement based messianic prophecies in the Bible. And I urge you to begin, or continue to study them out. Of course, statements are not the only way in which God generates prophecy. There are three other ways in which prophecies are introduced by God.

I JUST HAD THE MOST HELPFUL DREAM:
I WAS READING THE BIBLE AND PRAYING IN MY SLEEP! Hmm, I WONDER: DoES THAT COUNT AS QUALITY TIME WITH GOD?

2. Dreams

Despite the fact that we dream every night for our entire lives, dreams (prophetic or otherwise) have been baffling people since the beginning of time, and continue to do so. Early one morning, while it was still dark, I awoke and told my wife, "I just had the most helpful dream. I was reading the Bible and praying in my sleep! Hmm, I wonder: does that count as quality time with God?" She was too tired to answer, and what could anyone really say with any real authority about the meaning of dreams. After all, Genesis 40:8 explains that **"interpretations belong to God."**

Gratefully, God explains a number of more important dreams in the Bible, and therein he uses special dreams and dreamers as a vehicle to predict and announce future events. Think of these types of biblical dreams as prophetic dreams, where a prediction or fantastic vision comes to a person in their sleep, while dreaming. God sends the dream, and in some cases the meaning of the dream is very clear. No interpretation is necessary with Jacob's dream in Genesis 28 where he sees a stairway to heaven. Within the dream, God plainly speaks to Jacob and says in verse 14, **"All peoples on earth will be blessed through you and your offspring."** From this verse, we understand that the Messiah will be able to trace his lineage back to Jacob. This is why Matthew starts his gospel with the genealogy of Jesus, tracing Jesus' line from generation to generation all the way back to Jacob.

We also understand from the dream in Genesis 28 that **"all peoples"** will be blessed through the Messiah, Jacob's offspring. This worldwide access to Jesus was fulfilled and explained in Hebrews 5:9. **"... he [Jesus] became the source of eternal salvation for all who obey him."** The church isn't just confined to benefiting the Jewish nation. **"All who obey"** Jesus from any nation can be saved.

In a number of other prophetic dreams, such as the dream of the Babylonian King Nebuchadnezzar in Daniel 2, the meaning of the dream is not clear to the dreamer. Therefore God gives the ability to interpret the king's dream to one of his people: in this case Daniel the prophet. Daniel explains from the layered statue of gold, silver, bronze and iron in the dream that the Messiah will come and set up an eternal kingdom (the church) during the fourth kingdom from that point.

Daniel 2:44-45 **"In the time of those kings, the God of heaven will set up a kingdom that will never be destroyed, nor will it be left to another people. It will crush all those kingdoms and bring**

them to an end, but it will itself endure forever. This is the meaning of the vision of the rock cut out of a mountain, but not by human hands a rock that broke the iron, the bronze, the clay, the silver and the gold to pieces. The great God has shown the king what will take place in the future. The dream is true and the interpretation is trustworthy."

History proves this to be exactly right; after the Babylonian kingdom, came the Persian, Greek, and then Roman kingdom. This is precisely when Jesus had his ministry. He was born, died, resurrected, and gave the Holy Spirit all during the fourth kingdom: the Roman kingdom. Daniel's prediction takes place around 550 BC, and the apostle Peter ushered in this eternal kingdom in Acts 2 during the first gospel sermon at Pentecost. This took place around 33 AD, just like Daniel said it would with confidence: **"The dream is true and the interpretation is trustworthy."**

Similar to dreams, the third method of generating prophecy that God uses may be the wildest, most mysterious, and awe inspiring type of prophecy: visions.

3. Visions

Prophecy is revealed to a prophet while they are awake by using powerful imagery and language that only the prophet can experience, such as the visions throughout the book of Ezekiel. Often such visions are not completely explained. Yet the more your biblical knowledge and faith grows, the more you will get the sense that God is giving you a prelude to deeper truths of his kingdom.

Many in the Christian religious world might cry "blasphemy" if I said that someone other than Jesus first bore the sins of the house of Israel. Yet turn to Ezekiel 4:4. **"Then lie on your left side and put the sin of the house of Israel upon yourself. You are to bear their sin for the number of days you lie on your side."**

What is going on here? In Ezekiel 4, the prophet has a vision of the **"son of man"** bearing the sins of all the people just outside of Jerusalem, and this while his arms are being bound and restrained. Sounds like we're describing Jesus, doesn't it? But in context, it's also visionary instruction for the prophet Ezekiel to go and do personally. In fact, 93 times (beginning with Ezekiel 2:1) throughout the entire book, the prophet Ezekiel is addressed as **"son of man."**

That's exactly what Jesus calls himself (or is referred to) a total of 82 times in the New Testament.

For a "son of man" example, most parallel to the cross, see Luke 24:7. Referring to Jesus, while at the empty tomb, two angels told the women that **"The Son of Man must be delivered into the hands of sinful men, be crucified and on the third day be raised again."**

The more you read, the more you realize that God was intricately involved in Ezekiel's life as a painful yet faithful foreshadowing of things to come. Visionary prophecy is a beacon traveling from the past to shine on the spectacular light of Jesus the Christ.

Another example includes the vision of the rivers flowing from God's temple in Ezekiel 47:1, 5, 9, and 12. **"The man brought me back to the entrance of the temple, and I saw water coming out from under the threshold of the temple.... He measured off another thousand, but now it was a river that I could not cross, because the water had risen and was deep enough to swim in--a river that no one could cross.... where the river flows everything will live.... Fruit trees of all kinds will grow on both banks of the river. Their leaves will not wither, nor will their fruit fail. Every month they will bear, because the water from the sanctuary flows to them. Their fruit will serve for food and their leaves for healing."**

This refreshing vision carries strong references to the pouring out of the Holy Spirit, God giving new life, the establishment of the church and its worldwide expansion, immersion in water (baptism), and the freshness of the gospel bearing fruit while continually healing lost souls (**"every month"**).

4. Events

A prophetic event is a historical event with overwhelming parallels to a different but related event in the future. The past event always has a double meaning; the first meaning relates directly to the particular events of that time, and the second and more profound meaning prophetically foreshadows a future event or fact. An example of this can be seen in the strong correlation between Abraham's near sacrifice of his son Isaac in Genesis 22 and God's sacrifice of his son Jesus roughly 2000 years later.

Genesis 22:1-2 **"Some time later God tested Abraham. He said to him, 'Abraham!' 'Here I am,' he replied. Then God said, 'Take your son, your only son, Isaac, whom you love, and go to the region of Moriah. Sacrifice him there as a burnt offering on one of the mountains I will tell you about.'"**

The parallels are already mounting up with the cross in just the first two verses. Isaac is Abraham's only son with Sarah, born to them when Abraham was 100 years old. The couple waited a long time for this promised child, just like God's people waited a long time for the coming of Jesus.

Also like Jesus, this only son Isaac is to be sacrificed in **"the region of Moriah... on one of the mountains."** In 2 Chronicles 3, we learn that the area where Isaac was to be sacrificed is later known as Jerusalem, on the very spot where God's temple gets built.

2 Chronicles 3:1 **"Then Solomon began to build the temple of the LORD in Jerusalem on Mount Moriah, where the LORD had appeared to his father David. It was on the threshing floor of Araunah the Jebusite, the place provided by David."**

The symmetry of these events is amazing. Isaac is almost sacrificed about 2000 BC. Then one thousand years later, in the same location, God's temple (where sacrifices are made) gets built. To complete the symmetry, in the same location, another one thousand years later, Jesus gets sacrificed. That's our mighty God, ordering life in a most symbolic, poetic, and unforgettable manner.

There is so much more to the historical and sacrificial depth of this location. Combining 2 Chronicles 3:1 (which ties Mount Moriah to the threshing floor of Araunah), with 2 Samuel 24 (where David sinned by counting the fighting men), we find that Mount Moriah is also the spot where an angel almost destroyed Jerusalem--yet God has mercy--and then King David builds an altar to the LORD on the threshing floor of Araunah. Again, that's the same spot Isaac was to be sacrificed, and the same area wherein Jesus really was sacrificed.

2 Samuel 24:15-19 **"So the LORD sent a plague on Israel from that morning until the end of the time designated, and seventy thousand of the people from Dan to Beersheba died. When the angel stretched out his hand to destroy Jerusalem, the LORD was grieved because of the calamity and said to the angel**

62

who was afflicting the people, 'Enough! Withdraw your hand.' The angel of the LORD was then at the threshing floor of Araunah the Jebusite. When David saw the angel who was striking down the people, he said to the LORD, 'I am the one who has sinned and done wrong. These are but sheep. What have they done? Let your hand fall upon me and my family.' On that day Gad went to David and said to him, 'Go up and build an altar to the LORD on the threshing floor of Araunah the Jebusite.' So David went up, as the LORD had commanded through Gad."**

Something David says here deserves more attention. Let's take a closer look at a prophetic statement in 2 Samuel 24:17 that David declares to God: **"Let you hand fall upon me and my family."** Despite the one thousand year timespan between David and Jesus' birth, Jesus is regarded as part of David's family and is even called **"the son of David"** a total of 16 times in the New Testament (Matthew 1:1, etc.). Therefore, at the cross, the hand of God does fall on David's family--through Jesus' crucifixion.

Getting back to the sacrifice of Isaac, we also find an overture of the resurrection.

Genesis 22:3-5 **"Early the next morning Abraham got up and saddled his donkey. He took with him two of his servants and his son Isaac. When he had cut enough wood for the burnt offering, he set out for the place God had told him about. On the third day Abraham looked up and saw the place in the distance. He said to his servants, 'Stay here with the donkey while I and the boy go over there. We will worship and then we will come back to you.'"**

Notice that Abraham, already expecting to sacrifice Isaac, still tells his servants that **"we [him and his son] will come back to you."** That's because Abraham believed that God would resurrect his son after the sacrifice. This is a most vivid foreshadowing of Jesus' resurrection, and one to call your faith higher. Abraham's faith in God went beyond life and death. No wonder he is considered a father in the faith.

Genesis 22:6-8 **"Abraham took the wood for the burnt offering and placed it on his son Isaac, and he himself carried** the fire and the knife. As the two of them went on together, Isaac spoke up and said to his father Abraham, 'Father?' 'Yes, my son?' Abraham replied. 'The fire and wood are here,' Isaac said, 'but where is the lamb for the burnt offering?' Abraham answered, 'God himself will provide the lamb for the burnt offering, my son.' And the two of them went on together."

Still completely intending to carry out the sacrifice of his son, what Abraham says here is exceedingly prophetic. He says **"God himself will provide the lamb for the burnt offering, my son."** Clearly, Abraham is looking beyond his own son's sacrifice and referring specifically to Jesus, **"the lamb of God who takes away the sin of the world!"** (John 1:29)

For anyone thinking that Abraham knew all along that his son would be spared, see Genesis 22:9-10. **"When they reached the place God had told him about, Abraham built an altar there and arranged the wood on it. He bound his son Isaac and laid him on the altar, on top of the wood. Then he reached out his hand and took the knife to slay his son."**

Whatever internal emotional struggles he might have had in carrying this sacrifice out, Abraham was fully resolved **"to slay his son."**

Genesis 22:11-14 **"But the angel of the LORD called out to him from heaven, 'Abraham! Abraham!' 'Here I am,"** he replied. **'Do not lay a hand on the boy,' he said. 'Do not do anything to him. Now I know that you fear God, because you have not withheld from me your son, your only son.' Abraham looked up and there in a thicket he saw a ram caught by its horns. He went over and took the ram and sacrificed it as a burnt offering instead of his son. So Abraham called that place The LORD Will Provide. And to this day it is said, 'On the mountain of the LORD it will be provided.'"**

The ram's head was caught in a thicket (branches interwoven) just as Jesus' head was caught in the crown of thorns (Matthew 27:29). These event parallels are way beyond coincidence. God substituted a ram in place of Isaac as an acceptable sacrifice. In the same way, to pay the price for our sin, Jesus was substituted for us at the cross. God provided for us through Jesus. Therefore even today, we can say with confidence, **"On the mountain of the LORD it will be provided."**

Genesis 22:15-18 **"The angel of the LORD called to Abraham from heaven a second time and said, 'I swear by myself, declares the LORD, that because you have done this and have not withheld your son, your only son, I will surely bless you and make your descendants as numerous as the stars in the sky and as the sand on the seashore. Your descendants will take possession of the cities of their enemies, and through your offspring all nations on earth will be blessed, because you have obeyed me.'"**

Abraham's faith and obedience leads to God's blessing for us-- even today. God basically tells Abraham that through his **"offspring"** (Jesus), all nations on earth will have access to God's blessing.

Is this not an event based prophecy to inspire faith and obedience throughout the ages? Classifying prophecy by four different types (Statements, Dreams, Visions and Events) provides additional usefulness for teaching purposes. Consider the particular backgrounds and interests of the people you are reaching out to. All biblical prophecies are powerful (showing the all-knowing and inspiring nature of God), but let's say you are reaching out to someone with more of an arts background. Which type of prophecy might have more of an impact? I would try some of the vision or dream based prophecies.

For the more orderly or linear minded people (self not included), such as accountants and perhaps those with a science background, try the statement based prophecies first. Which type might be memorable to an action focused sports fan? Try the event based prophecies first.

These four classifications of prophecy are also helpful in understanding how diversely creative and thorough God is at making sure we get his message in an unforgettable format. We should expect no less from our God almighty.

Now let's go to what I would call one of the most underrated examples of prophecy in the entire Bible. See if you can figure out which of the four types of prophecy it is: statement, dream, vision or event.

The action takes place somewhere in the forty year period between when the Israelites made their exodus from Egypt, but before they all crossed the Jordan and conquered the Promised Land. This is after their first attempt to take the Promised Land had failed, due to 10 of their 12 spies losing faith. It's a refining period of the Israelites' wandering in the desert. Moses' is moving on after the passing of two of his siblings. Miriam has recently died. Aaron has just been buried as well. And so we pick up in the Sinai Peninsula, a tract of land just southwest of the modern day border of Israel, outside of the Promised Land.

Numbers 21:4-9 The Bronze Snake Incident

4 **"They traveled from Mount Hor along the route to the Red Sea, to go around Edom. But the people grew impatient on the way;**

5 **they spoke against God and against Moses, and said, 'Why have you brought us up out of Egypt to die in the desert? There is no bread! There is no water! And we detest this miserable food!'**

6 **Then the LORD sent venomous snakes among them; they bit the people and many Israelites died.**

7 **The people came to Moses and said, 'We sinned when we spoke against the LORD and against you. Pray that the LORD**

will take the snakes away from us.' So Moses prayed for the people.

8 The LORD said to Moses, 'Make a snake and put it up on a pole; anyone who is bitten can look at it and live.'

9 So Moses made a bronze snake and put it up on a pole. Then when anyone was bitten by a snake and looked at the bronze snake, he lived."

Do you know which mode of prophecy this is? The first time I read this account of the bronze snake in Numbers 21, prophecy was the furthest thing from my mind. Instead, I thought three things about this poisonous snake attack.

1) This is bizarre and horrifying.

2) I'm glad I wasn't around back then for such chaos.

3) Other than that warning not to grumble, the story has nothing practical for me to use, so I might as well move on and forget it.

Of course that last line of thinking was foolish on my part. 1 Corinthians 10:6 explains that Old Testament events were written to teach us how to avoid evil today. **"Now these things occurred as examples to keep us from setting our hearts on evil things as they did."**

Despite this truth, as a young Christian, I quickly put this Old Testament snake attack episode behind me, dismissing it entirely. Then about a year later, I noticed something very curious about what Jesus said in John 3:14-16. **"Just as Moses lifted up the snake in the desert, so the Son of Man must be lifted up, that everyone who believes in him may have eternal life. For God so loved the world that he gave his one and only Son, that whoever believes in him shall not perish but have eternal life."**

Jesus is saying here that there is some sort of direct relationship between a desert snake and himself. It sounds almost like blasphemy. So I needed to take a closer look at Numbers 21 and soon discovered how those events are purposefully parallel to the cross.

Numbers 21 Outline

- The people sin and reject God (v. 5).
- Death is the consequence of sin (v. 6).

- The people ask to be saved (v. 7) while still guilty of sin.
- Alone, the leader prays to God for salvation... freedom from death for his people (v. 7).
- God provides a plan and instructions on how to be saved (v. 8) while many still die of their sin.
- After being refined by fire, the body, as a representation of sin and punishment, is lifted up for public display and hung on a pole (v. 9).
- The helpless and dying sinners who focus on the body hung on the pole will live and not be fatally punished for their own sin (v. 9).

Now what did I just describe: the incident of the bronze snake or the crucifixion of Jesus Christ? The answer is actually both. This is the essence of event based messianic prophecy; past events become forerunners of significant events in Jesus' day. The two events become connected by uncanny parallels that could only have been orchestrated by God.

The account of the bronze snake is one of the most vivid examples of predictive allusion in the whole Bible. It accurately points to the culminating event of Jesus' sacrifice for our sins on the cross, fourteen hundred years before it happened. Rereading the above outline of Numbers 21, it sounds like an exact outline of the account of the cross.

That's precisely God's plan, and just in case we were dull, Jesus even points us back to this in John 3 by saying, **"Just as Moses lifted up the snake in the desert, so the son of man must be lifted up."** This should leave no doubt that the making of this bronze snake from Numbers 21 alludes to Jesus being lifted up on a cross as God's solution to atone for the poisonous sins that would otherwise have left us for dead and without hope of rescue in the wilderness.

In fact, the Bible even goes further about the magnitude of this sacrifice and says that Jesus became sin to save us in 2 Corinthians 5:21. **"God made him** [Jesus] **who had no sin to be sin for us, so that in him we might become the righteousness of God."**

The author of life switched places with us. Jesus became sin instead of us, who rightly deserved it. That's a radical concept, tying mercy, the bronze snake, and the death of Jesus even closer together. In 2 Corinthians 5:21, Jesus becomes sin and is lifted up on a pole to deter the death of his people, just as the bronze snake is lifted on a pole in Numbers 21:9 to deter the death of God's people.

Remember that sin came into the world through the deceitfulness of the serpent from Genesis 3. Therefore implication of the snakes in Numbers 21 takes on an additionally profound meaning. God's people become more and more conscious about the deadliness of sin. Associating the deceiving serpent from Eden with the bronze snake and finally with Jesus, who never sinned, yet became sin, is most disturbing.

If relating Jesus on the cross to a snake unnerves you, then that's good. That's a main part of the point. We should be **"cut to the heart"** (Acts 2:37) over what we did to Jesus. Christ not only became sin on the cross, but he also became **"a curse for us,"** as stated in Galatians 3:13. **"Christ redeemed us from the curse of the law by becoming a curse for us, for it is written: 'Cursed is everyone who is hung on a tree.'"**

This is ugly, snake infested business the Lord got into for our sake. Yet it is out of this ugly, grim reality that we must grow to appreciate the magnitude and the mercy of God. Jesus gives us hope and a future through the cross. His resurrection makes our resurrection possible.

In essence, with the incident of the bronze snake, God allowed his people to experience a preview of the cross centuries before the actual happening. No such history of any other people is filled with such depth and truth. It's an action-packed event based prophecy that should make us grateful that we don't have to be bitten by snakes or hung on a cross to be saved. We just have to faithfully obey the Lord Jesus.

For me, biblical events can become more meaningful and memorable when I have a sense of what else was going on in the world at that time. Around the same period as the bronze snake (1440 BC), the following other events were happening:

The Arameans developed their language that dominated Syria and the surrounding area for centuries: Aramaic. Later, Jesus himself spoke this language while praying **"Abba"** (Father), in the garden of

Gethsemane (Mark 14:36). He also said one of his most chilling statements in Aramaic; **"My God, my God, why have you forsaken me?"** while suffering on the cross (Mark 15:34).

Other things going on in the world during the 15th Century BC include...

In India and Pakistan, the Battle of the Ten Kings takes place. This is recorded in the Rigveda, which is one of the four Hindu texts that they consider as sacred.

The Myceneans conquer Greece, a land that wouldn't become the major world kingdom described in Daniel for another one thousand years.

Central Europeans were burying their dead beneath burial mounds, also known as tumuli.

Fighting a coalition of Canaanite kings, Egypt defeats the Canaanites and extends control of their empire to include Canaan. Taking place just before the Israelite exodus, this was known as the Battle of Megiddo. It's one of the first well documented battles in history that records the number of killed soldiers (83) and the number captured (340).

The Egyptians were also digging the already 1000 year old Great Sphinx of Giza out of the desert sands which had buried it over time. In case you aren't up on Egyptian history, this Sphinx is a gigantic statue of a lion with the head of a human. It still exists today.

The Chinese were developing a writing system and bronze metallurgy. Their capital city at Ao had defense walls that were 65 feet thick at the base.

Both the Egyptians and the Chinese were practicing some shocking burial rituals. Their kings and queens were typically buried with all of their possessions, including all of their living servants. This was in preparation for their warped view of the afterlife, where they thought such possessions would be needed.

All these activities were taking place in the same century, while in the deserts just south of Canaan, God was preparing his people... training his people to recognize a savior that they would not see face to face for another fourteen hundred years. And 3500 years later, Christians today say with certainty, "Thank you God," and "Amen."

For some of the more historically minded people, you might be wondering, "So whatever happened to that bronze snake?" The reason why we can't see this object today lies in 2 Kings 18:3-4. This takes place about 700 years after Moses made the bronze snake. Joshua, King David, and King Solomon have long been dead. Isaiah the prophet is actively preaching at this time and we find that King Hezekiah **"did what was right in the eyes of the LORD, just as his father David had done. He removed the high places, smashed the sacred stones and cut down the Asherah poles. He broke into pieces the bronze snake Moses had made, for up to that time the Israelites had been burning incense to it..."**

On one hand, we can say, "That's awesome that a fired-up king went about the kingdom cleaning house and turning people back to God." But on the other hand, how sad it is to discover that the very tool God used to save his people from poisonous snakes had quickly degraded into another one of the Israelites' ungodly idols. This is a strong lesson on how easily religious based traditions of men can creep in and nullify the good workings of God.

Let that be a warning to well-meaning religious people today. Belief systems that have their origins in something godly do not make the whole belief system godly. Deviations from the original biblical intent, sincere or not, can quickly degenerate into a sinful tradition that needs to be smashed, cut down, and **"broke into pieces."**

Jesus sharply warns against traditions in Matthew 15:6-9. **"...Thus you nullify the word of God for the sake of your tradition. You hypocrites! Isaiah was right when he prophesied about you: 'These people honor me with their lips, but their hearts are far from me. They worship me in vain; their teachings are but rules taught by men.'"**

Traditions of men aside, understood properly as a messianic prophecy about the cross, the account of the bronze snake should build your faith in the continuity of the Bible and the incredible mercy of God. Making the connection from John 3:14, where Jesus predicts his being lifted up on the cross back to the account of the bronze snake should also make the following Scripture come to life even more.

2 Timothy 3:16 **"All Scripture is God-breathed and is useful for teaching, rebuking, correcting and training in righteousness"**

What's written about is the usefulness of the whole Bible: "All Scripture," not just your favorite verses from our "First Principles Study Series for Making Disciples." That, of course, is a phenomenal series, and it helps me every time I go through it. However, we can't stop there. We should be able to use every book of the Bible to teach, correct, etc. Practically speaking, when was the last time you taught someone using the book of Numbers? Can you prove to someone that Jesus is the Messiah by just using the Old Testament? Jesus can and did. See Luke 27:24. **"And beginning with Moses and all the Prophets, he** [Jesus] **explained to them what was said in all the Scriptures concerning himself."**

Notice in the above verse that Jesus is able to use the entire Old Testament in illustrating his divinity. We need to imitate Jesus and have purposeful Bible study specifically into the messianic prophecies.

My challenge for you is fourfold:

1) Scour the Old Testament for convincing proofs that Jesus is the Christ.

2) Find at least one example of each of the four types of prophecy

3) Memorize at least two of your favorite prophecies.

4) Teach them to each other and to the lost.

Chapter 11: Amos on the Messiah

In this lesson we will learn how to identify a messianic prophecy, particularly some of the lesser known prophecies in a lesser read book of the Bible--one that most people have a hard time finding without a table of contents.

We are doing this for two reasons:

1) To build your faith in the power of God and his word

2) To equip you with tools to deepen your Bible study

Unpack your spiritual shovels. We're going on a search for the Lord.

We have a large advantage today over those who lived prior to the completion of the New Testament. In less than a week, any one of us can readily read some or even all of the four Gospels and Acts. What is the big deal about these books? They are the fulfillment of happenings that Old Testament prophets had longed to see.

In Matthew 13:17, Jesus explains this to his disciples. **"For I tell you the truth, many prophets and righteous men longed to see what you see but did not see it, and to hear what you hear but did not hear it."**

For centuries, spiritual men, women, and children yearned for God to send a powerful shepherd king to rescue them from captivity and oppression. Those fully in tune with the prophecies were expecting nothing less than salvation from God himself.

When we speak of messianic prophecy, we are talking about truly great expectations. We are talking about an anointed Israelite man who turns out to actually be the creator, judge and savior of mankind. We are talking about Jesus Christ.

Therefore it can benefit you greatly to know the life of Jesus, the Messiah. Read the Gospels and pay attention to the details that God has put in there. It is much easier to see the messianic prophecies if you know what you are seeking. God guarantees that the seeker will be rewarded. As the Scripture says, **"...seek and you will find"** (Luke 11:9).

However, if you are anything like me, being a very slow reader and more of a visual learner, there are things you can do to speed your study along. Getting the Bible as a digital audio file can help you cover a lot of ground quickly, giving you a fluid overview of God's narrative to us. Books of the Bible can also be found on video as DVDs and some are even free for viewing on the Internet through YouTube. I know of at least three DVDs that are word for word live action narrations of the Bible. This includes the book of Matthew, Acts and John.

These multimedia tools are not substitutes for your Bible reading. Rather view them as supplements to your understanding of God. As mentioned earlier, many of these tools can be found for free. For example, if you have an MP3 player, you can download books of the Bible for free on the Internet and listen to them while traveling, or in place of TV time.

Note that the NIV translation of the Bible is generally not available as a free audio download, but there are many free options. A decent audio translation called the World English Bible is free to download and just as easy to understand.

Filing these study tools within our spiritual toolbox, let's now go straight into a biblical quest for messianic prophecy. In the 24 hour period leading up to Jesus' murder, we find a curious incident taking place in Mark 14:50-52 right after Jesus is arrested. **"Then everyone deserted him** [Jesus] **and fled. A young man, wearing nothing but a linen garment, was following Jesus. When they seized him, he fled naked, leaving his garment behind."**

Could this have been prophesied anywhere in the Old Testament? Why would such an odd detail even be important? Let's check this against Amos 2:16? **"Even the bravest warriors will flee naked on that day..."**

Fleeing and nakedness are mentioned here in both Mark and Amos, but that alone won't make it a messianic prophecy. Taking one isolated Old Testament verse and tying it to the cross should not be done lightly. We shouldn't jump to conclusions and declare this alone as a messianic prophecy... yet.

The best way to determine if a verse is prophetic is to keep reading and take a mental note of any other parallels that might come up. As you read Amos, the question to ask is this: "When Amos says, **'on that day'** in the passage we just read, what day is Amos talking about?" Read the entire book and find out what else God reveals about "that day."

If the composite picture painted by the multitude of prophecies can be applied to someone other than Jesus, then it's not a messianic prophecy. Conversely, if the material God reveals in prophecy only makes sense when overlaying it with the events of Jesus' life, then it must be about the Messiah.

As we read further in Amos, these are the things to keep in mind. In Amos 5:17, we find that God himself will be pass through among the people of the land for a brief period, yet the people will be engaged in widespread crying. **"'There will be wailing in all the vineyards, for I will pass through your midst,' says the LORD."**

This is starting to sound a little more like the day of Jesus' death. The amount of wailing is huge in conjunction with the events surrounding Jesus' death.

1) Peter **"wept bitterly"** when the rooster crowed on the third time that he denied Jesus (Matthew 26:75).

2) Judas **"was seized with remorse"** and ultimately hung himself over his betrayal of Jesus (Matthew 27:3-5).

3) Pilot's wife **"suffered a great deal"** in a dream because of Jesus (Matthew 17:19).

4) Jesus' followers **"mourned and wailed"** for Jesus on the way to being crucified (Luke 23:28).

5) Just before the moment of his own death on the cross, Jesus **"cried out again in a loud voice"** (Matthew 27:50).

6) Three days later before they knew of his resurrection, his disciples were still **"mourning and weeping"** (Mark 16:10).

7) Mary Magdalene cried extensively when she saw the empty tomb, and thought someone had stolen Jesus' body (John 20:11).

Clearly, Amos' prophecy about much wailing and the passing through of God fits perfectly with the events of cross.

Continuing on in Amos 5:22, more messianic activity unfolds; the former sacrificial system is rejected. **"Even though you bring me burnt offerings and grain offerings, I will not accept them..."**

God's rejection of bread and animal sacrifices makes way for the more perfect sacrifice: the body and blood of Jesus. Hebrews 10:11-14 explains this. **"Day after day every priest stands and performs** his religious duties; again and again he offers the same sacrifices, which can never take away sins. But when this priest had offered for all time one sacrifice for sins, he sat down at the right hand of God. Since that time he waits for his enemies to be made his footstool, because by one sacrifice he has made perfect forever those who are being made holy."

It doesn't get more perfect than that. Jesus' one sacrifice for sins was offered for all time. The Messiah is super-thorough and incomparably effective.

Continuing on to predictions in Amos, we come to a mother-load of prophecy in Amos that conclusively depicts the events surrounding the cross. See if you can spot five more references to Jesus' death below from Amos 8:8-11.

8 "'Will not the land tremble for this, and all who live in it mourn? The whole land will rise like the Nile; it will be stirred up and then sink like the river of Egypt.

9 In that day,' declares the Sovereign LORD, 'I will make the sun go down at noon and darken the earth in broad daylight.

10 I will turn your religious feasts into mourning and all your singing into weeping. I will make all of you wear sackcloth and shave your heads. I will make that time like mourning for an only son and the end of it like a bitter day.

11 The days are coming,' declares the Sovereign LORD, 'when I will send a famine through the land--not a famine of food or a thirst for water, but a famine of hearing the words of the LORD.'"

What a difficult time this must have been. Let's outline the events.

Verse 8: There's an earthquake on the same day that...

Verse 9: ...the sky goes dark at noon...

Verse 10: ...during a religious feast...

Verse 10: ...as there is mourning for an only son and...

Verse 11: ...the people will be completely without God's word (famine) for a number of days.

Did we just describe Amos 8 or the exact conditions surrounding the death of Jesus? The answer of course, is both, especially after reading Matthew 27:45-54.

45 "From the sixth hour until the ninth hour darkness came over all the land.

46 About the ninth hour Jesus cried out in a loud voice, 'Eloi, Eloi, lama sabachthani?'--which means, 'My God, my God, why have you forsaken me?'

47 When some of those standing there heard this, they said, 'He's calling Elijah.'

48 Immediately one of them ran and got a sponge. He filled it with wine vinegar, put it on a stick, and offered it to Jesus to drink.

49 The rest said, 'Now leave him alone. Let's see if Elijah comes to save him.'

50 And when Jesus had cried out again in a loud voice, he gave up his spirit.

51 At that moment the curtain of the temple was torn in two from top to bottom. The earth shook and the rocks split.

52 The tombs broke open and the bodies of many holy people who had died were raised to life.

53 They came out of the tombs, and after Jesus' resurrection they went into the holy city and appeared to many people.

54 When the centurion and those with him who were guarding Jesus saw the earthquake and all that had happened, they were terrified, and exclaimed, 'Surely he was the Son of God!'"

Breaking down the death of Jesus in Matthew 26 and 27 brings remarkable parallels with Amos.

Matthew 26:2 - Jesus dies during a religious feast.

"As you know, the Passover is two days away--and the Son of Man will be handed over to be crucified."

Matthew 27:45 - Darkness at noon

"The sixth hour" in Jewish timekeeping refers to noon.

Matthew 27:50 - A three-day famine for hearing God's word starts because Jesus has just died.

Matthew 27:51, 52, 54 - Earthquake

"The earth shook... rocks split... tombs broke open... earthquake"

Matthew 27:54 - Son of God

The centurion exclaimed, **"Surely he was the Son of God!"**

Indeed, we are far past the point of coincidence between Amos and Matthew. We are looking at divine messianic prophecy. Aside from the main point that Jesus died for my sin, one of the points that also hits me deeply is the parallel between Amos' 8:11 prophecy about **"a famine of hearing the words of the LORD"** and the three days that Jesus was dead. How sad those days must have been. Jesus' closest friends must have longed for more of his wisdom, his truth, and grace. Yet the three days ticked quietly by with no word of hope.

This reminds me of the self-imposed "famine" that people create today for the word of God in their lives: how sad, how hopeless this is. How often in my life have I had a Bible within arm's reach, yet not appreciated or applied God's word? That's a famine.

Amos' prophecy about **"a famine of hearing the words of the LORD"** should not be an everyday prediction of our lives. It should be a one-time foretelling of the three wordless days that Jesus was in the tomb, and nothing more, because Jesus rose from the dead, preached much more, and now we use his word every day in our lives. We have the power to end the famine. No more starvation. Let's use God's word daily.

In Amos 9:8, God reveals even more about the coming of his kingdom.

"'Surely the eyes of the Sovereign LORD are on the sinful kingdom. I will destroy it from the face of the earth--yet I will not totally destroy the house of Jacob,' declares the LORD."

Here we see that a sinful kingdom will be destroyed by God, yet God will leave a remnant of Israelites. This makes way for the new spiritual kingdom to come: the church.

Then Amos 9:11-12 specifically describes the coming of Jesus' church with the phrase **"David's fallen tent."**

"In that day I will restore David's fallen tent. I will repair its broken places, restore its ruins, and build it as it used to be, so that they may possess the remnant of Edom and all the nations that bear my name..."

We can be certain that **"David's fallen tent"** refers to the new church because the disciple James describes it as such in Acts 15:16

and he even quotes Amos 9 to make the point that even the gentiles (all the nations) can be part of God's church.

Acts 15:13-19 **"When they finished, James spoke up: 'Brothers, listen to me. Simon has described to us how God at first showed his concern by taking from the Gentiles a people for himself. The words of the prophets are in agreement with this, as it is written: "After this I will return and rebuild David's fallen tent. Its ruins I will rebuild, and I will restore it, that the remnant of men may seek the Lord, and all the Gentiles who bear my name, says the Lord, who does these things" that have been known for ages. It is my judgment, therefore, that we should not make it difficult for the Gentiles who are turning to God.'"**

From the above passage we can see that David's fallen tent is pitched up again as the church of the first century. Disciples today can also share in this legacy: we are the new remnant who bear the name of the Lord.

It is so awesome to be reassured that God had a plan for all nations even from the days of Amos. Factoring in the messianic prophecies from all of Amos, the prophecies about Jesus in just the book of Amos look like this:

During a religious feast, men flee and there is nakedness. The long standing sacrificial system of animals and food offerings are rejected by God, leaving room for a new sacrifice. The earth gets dark at noon on the same day that there is an earthquake and widespread mourning for the only son. For days the people are even completely without the word of God. Sinful kingdoms are destroyed, but God leaves an Israelite remnant that will be restored and rebuilt into a new dwelling. This new home will include gentiles and all the members will bear God's name.

How much more parallel can we get? The book that most religious people rarely talk about contains the very plan that all people need to be a part of. Amos is talking about your only hope for salvation. He's talking about you going through Jesus as the only way to get back to God, and stay with him in his dwelling place, and in his name.

As we can see, Amos is more than a brand of cookies (Famous Amos), and so much more than an old-time radio show (Amos and Andy). Therefore, I have an Amos-like challenge for you. Pick another Old Testament book like Amos. Frankly it would be great to pick a book of the Bible that you are the least interested in, and scour it for one thing, and one thing alone: messianic prophecies. Find Jesus the Christ, and you will find **"the way and the truth and the life"** (John 14:6).

Chapter 12: Forsaken, But Why?

In the 1970s, when I was a kid, for many years my Dad would tell me, along with my brother and sisters, that in a few years he would bring us to an unpopulated island in the middle of nowhere and leave us there for one week. In this way, he explained with the esteemed intensity of a United States marine, his children would learn how to work together and survive off of the land.

Being so young and quite impressionable, my siblings and I had little recourse but to humbly accept the coming of our survivalist time of testing. My Dad would speak about this looming event as casually as one might talk about cutting the front lawn--as if this were an exercise that every good kid must soon endure.

When my dear Mother would try to interject about how my Dad was--of course--just joking, the resolve of my Father would remain unshaken. He simply replied, "This is good for them. Don't worry about it. That's how the people learn."

Consequently, I grew up half of my childhood years cherishing the precious moments before our potentially deadly island trials. I dreaded an unspecified, yet near-future when we would be shipped off to some deserted island where some of us may not survive.

Being a Vietnam War Veteran accustomed to surviving in the wild jungles of Asia, us kids all took our Dad completely seriously-- and it terrified us. Being abandoned--even for a little while--from our Father in such a remote, lonely place was a source of real anguish. I never wanted that moment to come. Who would want to be forsaken by their own Father?

Thankfully for me, that week never came. To this day, I don't know if Dad was bluffing or if he just forgot about his survival challenge for his offspring. We never did end up on any deserted island, and I thank God for that. Right or wrong, the experience taught me an unforgettable lesson; I would never want to be abandoned by my Father--not even if there was some greater good associated with it.

Previously, I had touched upon the concept of Jesus being forsaken for our benefit. The issue deserves deeper reflection. That God in the flesh became abandoned/forsaken is a vital and alarming biblical event that changes lives, once properly understood. The more I looked into it, the prophetic message of Psalm 22, with its prediction of the forsaken state of Jesus on the cross, became magnified into nothing less than shocking.

Psalm 22:1 **"My God, my God, why have you forsaken me? Why are you so far from saving me, so far from my cries of anguish?"**

Jesus says this exact phrase about one thousand years later in Matthew 27:46, while in the last stage of his suffering on the cross. **"About the ninth hour Jesus cried out in a loud voice, 'Eloi, Eloi, lama sabachthani?'--which means, 'My God, my God, why have you forsaken me?'"**

Jesus isn't simply quoting the Psalms here to play out his part in a theatrical production because he rehearsed this moment. No, not at all. In the agony of his punishment, Jesus really felt and thought these words. And these very words describing his status of being forsaken were predicted one thousand years prior. Why would a statement anyone would make be so important as to be predicted in the previous millennium? To fully appreciate what is going on here, we need to take a deeper look into what it means to be **"forsaken."**

From Strong's Lexicon reference #H5800, 'AZAB is the Hebrew word used for "forsaken" in Psalm 22:1. It's a verb that means "to leave, to let loose, to forsake, to abandon, to neglect, to be deserted." The same Hebrew word, 'AZAB, is used in Judges 10:13 to describe how God's people abandoned God; **"But you have forsaken me and served other gods, so I will no longer save you."**

Jesus felt abandoned on the cross because for a time, he was abandoned. In fact, he had to be abandoned for the salvation plan to work. The moment that Jesus cried, **"why have you forsaken me?"** was the moment when all of our sins were loaded upon him--perhaps even infused into his very mind and body. This is the moment when he became the bearer of our sins. Let me remind you that this is described in 2 Corinthians 5:21. **"God made him who had no sin to be sin for us, so that in him we might become the righteousness of God."**

Even though he never sinned, Jesus was made **"to be sin for us...."** Imagine living an innocent life, when suddenly all the dark

82

deeds of all humanity come crashing down into your very body. I liken it to a sweet and good-natured toddler being brought to the most gruesome horror movie ever and forced to sit through the whole film in the dark. This must have been completely overwhelming!

Despite the ugliness of sin, and separation from his father, Jesus participated willingly, and painfully at the cross. When Jesus died, he put our own punishment to death with him. He effectively paved the way for us to be pardoned from our own sin, taking on **"the punishment that brought us peace"** (Isaiah 53:5). That is our savior. That is our rescuer. That is our God!

In light of the multitude of prophecies and their fulfilments in the Bible, Jesus the Christ, **"the author and perfecter of our faith"** (Hebrews 12:2), has proven himself to be what he always has been: awesome and amazing. He forged our world and our creation. He endured our sin throughout the ages. He planned our redemption, predicted our rescue, and ultimately, suffered through that rescue mission by going through the cross for us.

Reflecting on the fullness of truths exposed through the prophecy of the Bible, these real Scriptures stand straight up in the test of time as the holy writings of the living God. The Bible has been set aside by God for us in the hope that we will set aside our lives for a relationship with God.

This relationship can grow as we gain a greater and greater confidence and appreciation for the only book that is **"living and active"** (Hebrews 4:12). Housed securely in the Bible, the real Scriptures stand up tall and have been calling out to us for centuries with unfailing accuracy, truth, and direction for our lives. One question remains for us to ponder until the end of our days; will we answer the call of Jesus the Christ?

Chapter 13: The Radical Relevance of the Old Testament

Recently I met with a dear friend who had become really confused about the Bible--so much so that he was about to leave the church and even give up on prayer. He said "I just can't believe the whole Bible because more than half of it--the Old Testament--is considered outdated. All that stuff isn't relevant anymore. After all, we're in the New Covenant."

Naturally, my internal alarm bells were going off at such a misguided and untrue statement. Yet I was also extremely grateful that my friend took the time to transparently articulate where he was at in his thinking--right or wrong. It gave me the precious opportunity to provide help.

We wasted no time in going to the "Old" Testament and seeing just how relevant it really was, and still is. Immediately, a study of the book of Isaiah was in order. After all, Isaiah is a fire hose of messianic prophecy, and something strong was needed to douse out the flames of faithlessness. It's actually harder to find chapters of Isaiah that *aren't* about Jesus than otherwise. Herein lies a sampling of some of Isaiah's advance views of Jesus the Messiah.

Isaiah 52:2-3 reads **"Shake off your dust; rise up, sit enthroned, O Jerusalem. Free yourself from the chains on your neck, O captive Daughter of Zion. For this is what the LORD says: 'You were sold for nothing, and without money you will be redeemed.'"**

It is predicted that God's people (Jerusalem/Daughter of Zion) will be **"redeemed"** from slavery (to sin) without money. This is exactly how Jesus bought us back. He did not pay for us with money. He paid for us on the cross with his own life. This is an act of courage designed to endear us to Jesus.

It is also very endearing to see that God wants his people to be free from the chains of sin. He has a deep interest in our personal freedom and is extremely active in the plan for us to be free. Yet as his followers, we have to want to be free. Some people are comfortable in their misery. They lack the courage to change with God's help. How badly do you want freedom? Are you willing to identify the areas in which you are still a slave to fear, arrogance, or other sins that can bind you like a slave?

We can be doubly sure this passage is talking about Jesus the more we read. Isaiah 52:8-10 says **"Listen! Your watchmen lift up their voices; together they shout for joy. When the LORD returns to Zion, they will see it with their own eyes. Burst into songs of joy together, you ruins of Jerusalem, for the LORD has comforted his people, he has redeemed Jerusalem. The LORD will lay bare his holy arm in the sight of all the nations, and all the ends of the earth will see the salvation of our God."**

The LORD is the one who **"returns"** to Jerusalem. The people **"will see"** this event **"with their own eyes,"** because Jesus came as God in the flesh. He has also **"comforted"** and **"redeemed."** How does God set such tasks in motion? As Jesus, **"the LORD will lay bare his holy arm"** and this leads to **"all the ends of the earth"** seeing **"the salvation of our God."** At the cross, God, as Jesus, laid **"bare his holy arm in the sight of all the nations"** as the nails were driven through him in public. The Lord was displayed as a gross spectacle before all the people.

Jesus laid bare his holy arm again so that Thomas, one of the doubters, could even touch Jesus' nail wounds after the resurrection in John 20:25-28. **"So the other disciples told him, 'We have seen the Lord!' But he said to them, 'Unless I see the nail marks in his hands and put my finger where the nails were, and put my hand into his side, I will not believe it.' A week later his disciples were in the house again, and Thomas was with them. Though the doors were locked, Jesus came and stood among them and said, 'Peace be with you!' Then he said to Thomas, 'Put your finger here; see my hands. Reach out your hand and put it into my side. Stop doubting and believe.' Thomas said to him, 'My Lord and my God!'"**

Thomas' experience can be so encouraging; there is hope for the doubters. I was one of those doubters in the past, and don't we all go through periods of doubt in our lives? Yet through the workings of God and the wealth of evidence about Jesus throughout the Bible, those days are over and done. I believe!

Isaiah 52:13-15 ramps up into more details about Jesus at the cross. **"See, my servant will act wisely, he will be raised and lifted up and highly exalted. Just as there were many who were appalled at him--his appearance was so disfigured beyond that of any man and his form marred beyond human likeness--so will he sprinkle many nations, and kings will shut their mouths because of him. For what they were not told, they will see, and what they have not heard, they will understand."**

Here we have God's **"servant"** who is **"raised and lifted up."** That's an accurate depiction of Jesus lifestyle of servitude and the process of him being hung up on a Roman cross. This same person who was crucified is also **"highly exalted."** In other words, Jesus' resurrection proves his supremely elevated position as he who conquered death and was given **"all authority in heaven and on earth"** (Matthew 28:18).

Isaiah 52:13-15 also correctly predicts the extreme physical mistreatment of Jesus leading up to the cross. The crowd was **"appalled with him--his appearance was so disfigured beyond that of any man and his form marred beyond human likeness."** The beating Jesus endured by the hands of the Roman soldiers was so terrible, it was shocking. By the end of the torture, Jesus was unrecognizable and barely looked human.

Isaiah 52:15 explains that Jesus' sacrifice will **"sprinkle many nations."** In other words, this is not just an Israelite salvation plan. By Jesus' blood, all nations have access to a saving relationship with God. The very act of Jesus' death, burial, and resurrection is so impressive and inspiring, that even **"kings will shut their mouths because of him."** The spreading of this gospel, as well as the changed lives and radical repentance of Jesus' disciples will help the kings of the earth **"see"** and **"understand"** that true Christianity is here to stay! It is a movement of God that every earthly kingdom must take seriously.

This of course leads us to Isaiah 53. It is one of the richest prophetic chapters on the cross in all the Bible. Entire books have been devoted to this one amazing chapter. That's how powerful it is. If you read the crucifixion account in the last three chapters of Matthew and then go back and read Isaiah 53 (written 750 BC), you will be stunned. The two accounts, though separated by about 850 years, are amazingly aligned with the blow-by-blow details of Jesus' death, burial, and resurrection. What follows is a verse by verse analysis of Isaiah 53.

Isaiah 53:1 **"Who has believed our message and to whom has the arm of the LORD been revealed?"**

The context is set by explaining that this account has to do with God revealing himself by his arm. There is also an implication that not everyone will believe this message, or at least that this message will cause many to question.

Isaiah 53:2 **"He grew up before him like a tender shoot, and like a root out of dry ground. He had no beauty or majesty to attract us to him, nothing in his appearance that we should desire him."**

Speaking about Jesus' upbringing, he is described as growing up **"tender."** This gently depicts how Jesus' birth gave him all the qualities of life that made him (and us) vulnerable. However, Jesus was also **"like a root out of dry ground."** In other words, while he was human, he was also the root, as in the source of life. That's what roots do; they support the rest of the plant. Jesus, the life source was also **"out of dry ground,"** meaning that his surrounding environment was spiritually dying. Think of an uprooted plant lying on a rock. No support would come from such a scenario--only dehydration and eventual death. Is this not the world we live in-- spiritually dying due to the rejection of God's word?

Verse 2 also mentions Jesus' appearance as unattractive and undesirable. If we take this passage as a continuation of Isaiah 52:14 (with his appearance **"so disfigured"**), then we see that we are indeed talking about Jesus at the cross. There's nothing majestic about an innocent man being mistreated to death.

Isaiah 53:3 **"He was despised and rejected by men, a man of sorrows, and familiar with suffering. Like one from whom men hide their faces he was despised, and we esteemed him not."**

Jesus was certainly **"despised and rejected by men."** Fulfilled in Matthew 27:22-23, all the crowd shouts out loud and repeated demands to **"crucify him!"** As an intentional understatement, the cross made Jesus quite "familiar with suffering." Men hid **"their**

faces" from him even to the point that all his disciples **"deserted him and fled"** (Matthew 26:56).

Isaiah 53:4 **"Surely he took up our infirmities and carried our sorrows, yet we considered him stricken by God, smitten by him, and afflicted."**

Jesus **"took up"** our sin on the cross. Romans 8:3 confirms the fulfillment of this, showing what **"...God did by sending his own Son in the likeness of sinful man to be a sin offering."** In Jesus' carrying of the cross, Isaiah 53:4 also prophesies that Jesus **"carried our sorrows."** To add insult to injury, the religious leaders mocked him by saying **"He trusts in God. Let God rescue him"** (Matthew 27:43). It shows how they **"considered him stricken"** and **"smitten"** by God.

Isaiah 53:5 **"But he was pierced for our transgressions, he was crushed for our iniquities; the punishment that brought us peace was upon him, and by his wounds we are healed."**

This 750 BC prediction that Jesus would specifically be **"pierced"** is more amazing when we realize that the practice of crucifixion was not a common form of execution at the time of Isaiah. Not until 519 BC, during the Persian Empire, is such a practice recorded in history as having taken place as an actual form of punishment. In the Behistun Inscription, by Darius the Great, column 3, lines 49 and 50 of the Inscription, it reads as follows:

"King Darius says: While I was in Persia and in Media, the Babylonians revolted from me a second time. A certain man named Arakha, an Armenian, son of Haldita, rebelled in Babylon.... Then I made a decree, saying: Let that Arakha and the men who were his chief followers be crucified in Babylon!"

The foreknowledge of God through his word in Isaiah 53:5 shows that piercing as punishment is coming into the world, and most gruesomely, to our savior. Jesus' punishment **"brought us peace"** because we do not have to be crucified for our sins. Jesus paid that price. As Isaiah 53:5 sums up, by Jesus' piercing **"wounds we are healed."** In light of all the nasty and barbaric details that can be discovered about the history of crucifixions, we have so much to be grateful for. Jesus took that pain for us.

Isaiah 53:6 **"We all, like sheep, have gone astray, each of us has turned to his own way; and the LORD has laid on him the iniquity of us all."**

Mentioned again is the prophecy that all Jesus' entire nation, including his own disciples, have deserted him. In John 10:11, Jesus identifies himself as **"the good shepherd."** Like sheep, we too **"have gone astray."** We must personalize Jesus' courage to be sacrificed for us and bear our iniquity, since it applies to all people.

Isaiah 53:7 **"He was oppressed and afflicted, yet he did not open his mouth; he was led like a lamb to the slaughter, and as a sheep before her shearers is silent, so he did not open his mouth."**

This verse is exactly what Jesus did when questioned by the religious leaders after his arrest; **"he did not open his mouth"** to defend himself. Matthew 26:60-63 shows that **"though many false witnesses came forward... Jesus remained silent."** Sadly, the **"famine of hearing the words of the LORD"** that Amos 8:11 describes actually started just before Jesus death, due to Jesus' silence.

Jesus is also described in Isaiah 53:7 as **"a lamb to the slaughter."** This is exactly why John the Baptist called Jesus **"the lamb of God, who takes away the sin of the world,"** in John 1:29. John was picturing Jesus, not as a cuddly clean lamb that a person can snuggle with, but as an innocent human being brutally slaughtered. The cousin of Jesus understood Isaiah's gripping prophecy about the sacrificial character of Jesus. Let's make sure we do as well.

Isaiah 53:8 **"By oppression and judgment he was taken away. And who can speak of his descendants? For he was cut off from the land of the living; for the transgression of my people he was stricken."**

Being **"cut off from the land of the living"** clearly explains that Jesus would die, and indeed he did die and was buried in Matthew 27:50, 59-60. **"And when Jesus had cried out again in a loud voice, he gave up his spirit.... Joseph** [of Arimathia] **took the body, wrapped it in a clean linen cloth, and placed it in his own** new tomb that he had cut out of the rock. He rolled a big stone in front of the entrance to the tomb and went away."

Isaiah 53:9 **"He was assigned a grave with the wicked, and with the rich in his death, though he had done no violence, nor was any deceit in his mouth."**

Without knowing the facts of Jesus' death, this verse might seem like it contradicts itself. Yet being **"assigned a grave with the wicked, and with the rich in his death"** is exactly outlining the unique conditions of Jesus' death. Sentenced to the grave, he was crucified with two **"wicked"** robbers (Matthew 27:38). Then Joseph of Arimathia, wealthy enough to have his own **"new tomb,"** wrapped and buried Jesus' body there. Joseph is even described as **"a rich man"** in Matthew 27:57.

Isaiah 53:9 also accurately predicts Jesus' non-violent behavior. Throughout his entire ministry, **"he had done no violence."** Contrast this with Peter, in Matthew 26:51, who **"reached for his sword, drew it out and struck the servant of the high priest, cutting off his ear."** Despite being in the middle of his arrest and betrayal, Jesus even goes on to heal that dismembered ear in Luke 22:51.

Jesus' non-violent stance was not from a position of fear, but from a position of power, restraint, and trust in his Father. This is evident from what he said in Matthew 26:53. **"Do you think I cannot call on my Father, and he will at once put at my disposal more than twelve legions of angels?"** To get a sense of how many angels Jesus is talking about, the number of soldiers in just one Roman legion would be anywhere from 2,000 to 6,000 men. So Jesus is at least talking about 24,000 angels. That's a lot of power, showing Jesus' incredible amount of restraint under pressure.

Isaiah 53:10 **"Yet it was the LORD's will to crush him and cause him to suffer, and though the LORD makes his life a guilt offering, he will see his offspring and prolong his days, and the will of the LORD will prosper in his hand."**

Here is a reference to Jesus' death and resurrection all in one sentence. His life was made into **"a guilt offering."** This always meant death. Yet Jesus won't stay dead because **"he will see his offspring and prolong his days."**

Jesus sees over 500 of his **"offspring"** (disciples) after the resurrection in 1 Corinthians 15:3-6. Paul writes that **"...Christ died for our sins according to the Scriptures, that he was buried, that he was raised on the third day according to the Scriptures, and that he appeared to Peter, and then to the Twelve. After that, he appeared to more than five hundred of the brothers at the same time, most of whom are still living, though some have fallen asleep."**

Jesus didn't merely **"see"** his followers from a box seat in heaven. As the resurrected Messiah, he saw them face to face with his own eyes, and over 500 disciples peered back at him with their astounded eyes.

Isaiah 53:11 **"After the suffering of his soul, he will see the light** [of life] **and be satisfied; by his knowledge my righteous servant will justify many, and he will bear their iniquities."**

Here we have another mention of Jesus' resurrection. How sad it is to note that Jesus suffered in every way imaginable--even in **"his soul."**

Isaiah 53:12 **"Therefore I will give him a portion among the great, and he will divide the spoils with the strong, because he poured out his life unto death, and was numbered with the transgressors. For he bore the sin of many, and made intercession for the transgressors."**

Jesus' sacrifice is again described as resulting **"unto death,"** yet also greatness, and dividing **"the spoils with the strong."** That is the victory of the resurrection. We too will rise after death to be with him. Jesus didn't keep all the victory to himself. He shares it, or **"divides the spoils"** with his followers--the **"strong."** How are we strong? Certainly not by our own power, but by **"the Holy Spirit, whom God has given to those who obey him"** (Acts 5:32).

That's the entire chapter of Isaiah 53: a gold mine of messianic prophecy. Yet this chapter is not alone in preparing us to meet our savior. Moreover, it is certainly not the only chapter that holds a wealth of inspiring prophecy about the cross.

Isaiah 59:1-4 reads **"Surely the arm of the LORD is not too short to save, nor his ear too dull to hear. But your iniquities have separated you from your God; your sins have hidden his** face from you, so that he will not hear. For your hands are stained with blood, your fingers with guilt. Your lips have spoken lies, and your tongue mutters wicked things. No one calls for justice; no one pleads his case with integrity. They rely on empty arguments and speak lies; they conceive trouble and give birth to evil."

Look at repeated the use of the phrase **"arm of the LORD."** That arm--by being pierced--can save you, yet there's blood on your hands. You are responsible for the cross. There's also no justice, only lies. Is that not an accurate depiction of Jesus' treatment on the cross? A review of all the crucifixion accounts in the gospels confirms that no one **"pleads his case with integrity."** In fact, no one pleads Jesus' case at all.

Isaiah 59:9-10 aligns with more details of the crucifixion. **"So justice is far from us, and righteousness does not reach us. We look for light, but all is darkness; for brightness, but we walk in deep shadows. Like the blind we grope along the wall, feeling our way like men without eyes. At midday we stumble as if it were twilight; among the strong, we are like the dead."**

This prophecy accurately predicts Matthew 27:45, that the **"darkness came over all the land"** in the middle of the day when Jesus was hanging on the cross. The subsequent death of Jesus left people spiritually blind and spiritually **"like the dead,"** groping at our own wall of sin and **"feeling our way like men without eyes."**

Isaiah 59:12-13 shows our betrayal was against God himself. **"For our offenses are many in your sight, and our sins testify against us. Our offenses are ever with us, and we acknowledge our iniquities: rebellion and treachery against the LORD, turning our backs on our God, fomenting oppression and revolt, uttering lies our hearts have conceived."**

The **"turning our backs on our God"** is a grim yet true reference to our own rebellion as well as the original disciples who **"deserted him [Jesus] and fled,"** as fulfilled in Matthew 26:56.

Isaiah 59:16-17 repeats the theme that it is the literal arm of God that provides the saving intervention. **"He saw that there was no one, he was appalled that there was no one to intervene; so his own arm worked salvation for him, and his own righteousness**

92

sustained him. He put on righteousness as his breastplate, and the helmet of salvation on his head; he put on the garments of vengeance and wrapped himself in zeal as in a cloak."

How sad and gruesome it is that the original "helmet of salvation on his head" was a bloody crown of thorns. A prophetic reference to the crown of thorns is also cited in Isaiah 55:13. **"Instead of the thornbush will grow the pine tree, and instead of briers the myrtle will grow. This will be for the LORD's renown, for an everlasting sign, which will not be destroyed."**

Referring to the time when Jesus comes, two plants are contrasted. The thornbush, which was used to make the crown of thorns, had no significant human value. However the pine tree has so many uses and can be a great help to all people. The needles of certain pine trees contain nutrients. The wood of a pine is tall and straight, making it ideal for construction. Also pinecones, as well as sap from a pine tree are great fire starters. You can even make torches from pine tree sap.

The phrase **"for the LORD's renown, for an everlasting sign"** is remarkable. Roughly two thousand years after the fact, people are still talking about Jesus's crown of thorns. Artists frequently depict him wearing the cruel crown. Is this not something that God is renowned for, and an **"everlasting sign"** of what Jesus endured for us? Therefore the implication of this passage foreshadows how Jesus' coming will take us from the thorns of his painful punishment into an era of indestructible and nurturing security.

Getting back to Isaiah 59, verse 16 also accurately describes how **"there was no one to intervene"** at the cross. No one came to the rescue. Therefore, all Jesus had, before he died, was **"his own righteousness."**

The wrapping **"in zeal"** mentioned here in Isaiah 59 is evident in a most baffling way right after Jesus' death. Note the zealously wild happenings from Matthew 27:51-53. **"At that moment the curtain of the temple was torn in two from top to bottom. The earth shook and the rocks split. The tombs broke open and the bodies of many holy people who had died were raised to life. They came out of the tombs, and after Jesus' resurrection they went into the holy city and appeared to many people."**

93

Jesus' zeal is so powerful, it rocks the world and propels the holy dead to revival and public action! Is that what Jesus is doing in your life? Don't wait until you're dead to get zealous for Jesus. Get revived and take action now.

While much more time could be spent studying Isaiah, let's examine an even older prophet and see how relevant his words are, even to this day. In the ancient Middle East, around 1700 BC, there was a righteous and rich man, a great family man, who rapidly lost everything that most people put their security in:

1) He lost his riches.
2) All his children died unexpectedly.
3) His health deteriorated into a life of horrible suffering.
4) His wife was not supportive and even hostile toward God.
5) His friends turned against him.

This man was faced with the universal human decision; should he draw closer to God in times of intense struggle, or should he stumble away from God in bitter discouragement? Such was the dilemma of a man called Job, whose very name means "persecuted," according to Gesenius' Hebrew-Chaldee Lexicon. While enduring such persecution, Job had clarity to speak quite boldly about the Messiah. Even though Job's statements are some of the most ancient sayings in the Bible (and in all of ancient history), they still ring out a completely timely and true message to this very day.

Job 16:19-22 **"Even now my witness is in heaven; my advocate is on high. My intercessor is my friend as my eyes pour out tears to God; on behalf of a man he pleads with God as a man pleads for his friend. Only a few years will pass before I go on the journey of no return."**

Despite his brutal hardships, Job is confident about Jesus the advocate. An advocate is someone who pleads another's cause, an intercessor. Job had faith that Jesus, on high, was pleading with God the Father specifically on Job's behalf for Job's cause! Job even understood that this physical life was not permanent, and **"the journey"** after death was coming. Job was looking forward to the point of no return: after death, when he could be with Jesus forever.

Not coincidentally, centuries later, in 1 John 2:1 (King James Version), Jesus is identified as the advocate as well. **"My little**

94

children, these things write I unto you, that ye sin not. And if any man sin, we have an advocate with the Father, Jesus Christ the righteous:"

The advocate is also referred to as the Holy Spirit in multiple chapters of John's gospel (14, 15, and 16). Tying this all together, we learn that Jesus is the advocate, the Holy Spirit is a manifestation of Jesus, and he is our defender, helper, and friend. Job trusted in this. I believe it helped him get through the dark valleys of suffering.

Job 19:25-27 **"I know that my Redeemer lives, and that in the end he will stand upon the earth. And after my skin has been destroyed, yet in my flesh I will see God; I myself will see him with my own eyes--I, and not another. How my heart yearns within me!"**

Troubles would not stop Job from knowing that his **"Redeemer lives."** We see Job craving for close relationship with God. Job was sure about the victorious future of Jesus, and that after Job died and his **"skin has been destroyed,"** Job's **"flesh"** would see God. What century-spanning faith! Job was certain that Jesus would one day resurrect him. Job understands that he would be purchased back (redeemed) by God. This is what true followers of Jesus are counting on: being united after death with the Messiah, regardless of the physical trials of this life. Job is famous for his suffering and endurance through times of trouble. Yet as evident in what he said, Job is also known for his deep trust in God. Don't wait for Job-like troubles to have Job-like trust in God! Trust in the Messiah now.

Clearly, the Scriptures in both the Old and New Testaments are alive and well. Living and active, they are relevant to the point of providing radical revelation about who we are and who our mighty Messiah is. He is Jesus, the living Redeemer, as Job called him. And as Isaiah prophesied, his mighty arm **"is not too short to save!"**

Chapter 14: Zechariah Nails It

As the second to last book in the Old Testament, the book of Zechariah is bursting with messianic prophecy to make your faith sizzle with excitement. The name "Zechariah" means "Jehovah remembers." What we will find, when reading through the book, is that indeed, God does remember his predictions and promises. The rescue plan is not forgotten; it is coming through Jesus Christ. Here are some highlights from Zechariah that display the Messiah in his amazing characteristics.

Zechariah 1:16 **"Therefore, this is what the LORD says: 'I will return to Jerusalem with mercy, and there my house will be rebuilt...'"**

Having a double meaning, this rebuilding statement can be applied to the 516 BC rebuilding of the demolished temple at Jerusalem. More importantly, this statement can also be applied to the 33 AD resurrection of Jesus. God himself--as Jesus--says that he **"will return to Jerusalem"** after his crucifixion with a rebuilt (resurrected) body. Jesus confirms this in John 2.

John 2:19-22 **"Jesus answered them, 'Destroy this temple, and I will raise it again in three days.' The Jews replied, 'It has taken forty-six years to build this temple, and you are going to raise it in three days?' But the temple he had spoken of was his body. After he was raised from the dead, his disciples recalled what he had said. Then they believed the Scripture and the words that Jesus had spoken."**

At the cross, those who passed by mocked and insulted Jesus about this very statement: that he would destroy and then raise the temple (his body) in three days (Matthew 27:39-40). Despite the mocking consensus of the crowd, the destruction and raising of Jesus' body is exactly what happened and what was predicted--all the way back from the time of Zechariah in 520 BC.

Like those who passed by Jesus at the cross, I have lived too much of my life as a mocker. I didn't understand the Bible and would simply jump to rash conclusions based on emotional response rather than truth. Making fun of people who were wholeheartedly following God was second nature to me. This is such a dangerous and empty state of existence in which to operate in. I am so thankful that God used his modern-day messengers to look past my mocking and help me see who Jesus really is: the only lasting way for all of us to rebuild our lives.

Continuing in Zechariah 1:16-17, it also says **"'...And the measuring line will be stretched out over Jerusalem,' declares the LORD Almighty. 'Proclaim further: This is what the LORD Almighty says: 'My towns will again overflow with prosperity, and the LORD will again comfort Zion and choose Jerusalem.'"**

The **"measuring line"** is used nine times in the Old Testament. It always applies to God's measure of justice. This means a precise measure of mercy marked out for the faithful, yet also a painful measure of punishment for the wicked. This can best be seen in Isaiah 28.

Isaiah 28:16-17 **"So this is what the Sovereign LORD says: 'See, I lay a stone in Zion, a tested stone, a precious cornerstone for a sure foundation; the one who trusts will never be dismayed. I will make justice the measuring line and righteousness the plumb line; hail will sweep away your refuge, the lie, and water will overflow your hiding place.'"**

Jesus is the **"cornerstone"** in this prophesied rebuilding by God. As the expert builder, God uses a builder's tool--the measuring line-- to show that his measure of justice is the fair and perfect amount. That's why we need to trust in God. Those who do so **"will never be dismayed."**

The overflowing water is a reference to the flood in the days of Noah; no one has a **"hiding place"** from it as that water put to death the evil of the era. That water is also a prophecy about baptism, an act of faith (Colossians 2:12) wherein God justifies those who believe by having us spiritually put to death our old self and participate in the death of Jesus (Romans 6:1-4).

Therefore to trust God, we must learn to love God's measuring line. He will mark out the proper justice, mercy, and boundaries for our life. God does something very encouraging with his measuring line in Zechariah 2.

Zechariah 2:1-5 **"Then I looked up--and there before me was a man with a measuring line in his hand! I asked, 'Where are** you going?' He answered me, 'To measure Jerusalem, to find out how wide and how long it is.' Then the angel who was speaking to me left, and another angel came to meet him and said to him: 'Run, tell that young man, "Jerusalem will be a city without walls because of the great number of men and livestock in it. And I myself will be a wall of fire around it," declares the LORD, "and I will be its glory within."'"

God is marking out the boundary for the faithful; that's the church--the **"city without walls."** Here we have one of the most animated descriptions of how God sees his church functioning as his kingdom on earth: as God's glorious dwelling of the faithful with God operating as a protecting and refining "wall of fire around it." Who is not super-encouraged by that?

Zechariah 2:10-11 **"'Shout and be glad, O Daughter of Zion. For I am coming, and I will live among you,' declares the LORD. 'Many nations will be joined with the LORD in that day and will become my people. I will live among you and you will know that the LORD Almighty has sent me to you.'"**

Here the LORD is speaking and twice he says that **"I will live among you."** Curiously though, the second time the LORD says this, the LORD also adds that **"you will know that the LORD Almighty has sent me to you."** This last statement is a bit puzzling so please go back and read this passage carefully. Why (or how) could the LORD say that he (the LORD) is coming to live among the people, yet also say that the LORD Almighty has sent him? If he is the LORD, and he sends himself, why does he refer to the LORD Almighty as if he were the other person who sends him?

This puzzle is only solved in knowing that God is Jesus. Then it all makes perfect sense. What this passage is saying is that the LORD Jesus is coming to the people. The LORD Jesus will live among the people, and the LORD Almighty (also known as the Father) will send the LORD Jesus. So here we have one of the most insightful nuggets in all the Old Testament that the LORD has distinct manifestations. In other words, Jesus is God. Let's be grateful for his coming!

The Messiah is the Branch

Many times in the Old Testament, the Messiah is called **"the Branch."** This represents God's servant who brings new growth that will bear fruit for God. Zechariah mentions the Branch twice.

Zechariah 3:8-9 **"'Listen, O high priest Joshua and your associates seated before you, who are men symbolic of things to come: I am going to bring my servant, the Branch. See, the stone I have set in front of Joshua! There are seven eyes on that one stone, and I will engrave an inscription on it,' says the LORD Almighty, 'and I will remove the sin of this land in a single day.'"**

Here, in a rock-solid manner, the Branch is associated with God removing **"the sin of this land in a single day."** This, of course, is a prophecy about the atoning sacrifice of Jesus at the cross. The Branch (Jesus), also described as **"the stone,"** will be engraved by the LORD Almighty. So Jesus the stone has the word of God embedded into his very makeup. That's Jesus, the living word of God (John 1).

Rewinding a bit back to the very beginning of Zechariah 3, we get an intense view of the spiritual happenings going unseen in our lives.

Zechariah 3:1-4 **"Then he showed me Joshua the high priest standing before the angel of the LORD, and Satan standing at his right side to accuse him. The LORD said to Satan, 'The LORD rebuke you, Satan! The LORD, who has chosen Jerusalem, rebuke you! Is not this man a burning stick snatched from the fire?' Now Joshua was dressed in filthy clothes as he stood before the angel. The angel said to those who were standing before him, 'Take off his filthy clothes.' Then he said to Joshua, 'See, I have taken away your sin, and I will put rich garments on you.'"**

It's quite unsettling to see Satan's role played out so close to the high priest--on his right side! Satan's job is to accuse God's priests of their sin, bring discouragement, and distraction away from God. This must make us more alert to devilish schemes that try to unseat our faith.

Nevertheless, it is awesome to see the angel call on the LORD to rebuke Satan. This is what we all need to do: call on God to rebuke Satan far from our lives. Make sure your prayers are alert and specific about keeping you from the evil one, as demonstrated here and throughout the Bible (Matthew 6:13, etc.).

Joshua is described as **"a burning stick snatched from the fire."** Then his sin is taken away. This is so prophetic about what Jesus does for his faithful followers. He rescues his disciples from the brink of the destruction that is owed to us due to our own sin. In my own life, this is a proper account of my being "snatched from the fire" of my former evil ways.

Incidentally, true followers of Jesus should all be able to describe themselves as **"a burning stick snatched from the fire."** Those who retain a great attitude about God's rescue plan continually say "Thank you God for getting me out of that fire!" However, there are many who started on the path of Christianity who have lost sight of the cross' rescuing properties. Such people adopt a bitter attitude which cries out, "Why did you let me get burned in the first place, God? The key is staying grateful to Jesus for being snatched from the fires of hell in the first place. He stood in our place. He was accused. He suffered for our sake. Thank you, Jesus Christ--the Branch that doesn't burn up.

The Branch is also significantly described later in Zechariah. Still referring to the high priest Joshua (not the same Joshua who took Jericho centuries earlier), the prophecy explains that the Branch (the Messiah) will build the temple of the LORD. That's the coming of the church.

Zechariah 6:12-13 **"Tell him this is what the LORD Almighty says: 'Here is the man whose name is the Branch, and he will branch out from his place and build the temple of the LORD. It is he who will build the temple of the LORD, and he will be clothed with majesty and will sit and rule on his throne. And he will be a priest on his throne. And there will be harmony between the two.'"**

The Messiah will be priest and king, which is why **"there will be harmony between the two"** offices. This is a reference to the anointed office of God's priest, and the anointed office of the king.

100

That's Jesus, the majestic king of the Jews, king of kings, and high priest forever.

Isaiah also prophesies about the Branch. From his first mentioning, we find that the Branch is **"one man,"** and **"of the LORD."** It is also clear that people will want to be called by his name--as in Christians--because this one man can **"take away our disgrace."**

Isaiah 4:1-6 **"In that day seven women will take hold of one man and say, 'We will eat our own food and provide our own clothes; only let us be called by your name. Take away our disgrace!' In that day the Branch of the LORD will be beautiful and glorious, and the fruit of the land will be the pride and glory of the survivors in Israel. Those who are left in Zion, who remain in Jerusalem, will be called holy, all who are recorded among the living in Jerusalem. The Lord will wash away the filth of the women of Zion; he will cleanse the bloodstains from Jerusalem by a spirit of judgment and a spirit of fire. Then the LORD will create over all of Mount Zion and over those who assemble there a cloud of smoke by day and a glow of flaming fire by night; over all the glory will be a canopy. It will be a shelter and shade from the heat of the day, and a refuge and hiding place from the storm and rain."**

We can see here that the followers of the Branch **"will be called holy."** They are holy because the Branch **"will wash away the filth"** and **"cleanse the bloodstains"** of his people. That's a reference to spiritual washing in water through baptism and forgiveness of sins through Jesus Christ. Cleansing the bloodstains specifically is about removing our blood-guilt; we are all responsible for Jesus' blood shed on the cross. But Jesus can take away this blood-guilt through a life devoted to serving him in grace, truth, and deed.

It is also comforting to know from Isaiah's prophecy that the LORD is the protector. God creates for his people **"a cloud of smoke by day and a glow of flaming fire by night."** In other words, he will always be guarding those who are his! He will provide **"shelter and shade"** for his assembled followers. Jesus is our **"refuge and hiding place"** from the storms of life. I need that so much: a hiding place in Jesus. Of course, we all need that!

Isaiah later describes the Branch as the fruitful offspring of Jesse (the father of King David) and having the **"Spirit of the LORD."**

Isaiah 11:1-4 **"A shoot will come up from the stump of Jesse; from his roots a Branch will bear fruit. The Spirit of the LORD will rest on him--the Spirit of wisdom and of understanding, the Spirit of counsel and of power, the Spirit of knowledge and of the fear of the LORD--and he will delight in the fear of the LORD. He will not judge by what he sees with his eyes, or decide by what he hears with his ears; but with righteousness he will judge the needy, with justice he will give decisions for the poor of the earth. He will strike the earth with the rod of his mouth; with the breath of his lips he will slay the wicked."**

The Branch does not decide things **"by what he hears with his ears."** This is about Jesus judging, not with observable information or the outward appearance, but **"with righteousness."** Moreover, the Branch **"will strike the earth with the rod of his mouth"** and **"slay the wicked"** with **"the breath of his lips."** That's power reserved only for Jesus, who can speak things into existence, and whose word is **"sharper than any double-edged sword"** (Hebrews 4:12).

This chapter is bursting with messianic information. Reading it in its entirety gives you such a great view of Jesus and his glorious kingdom.

Isaiah 11:10 **"In that day the Root of Jesse will stand as a banner for the peoples; the nations will rally to him, and his place of rest will be glorious."**

The more Isaiah goes on in chapter 11 to describe the Branch, the more we get the distinct picture of the Branch being fully a man, yet also fully God. The Root of Jesse mentioned at the beginning of the chapter is the Branch and **"nations will rally to him."** The only person in all of history to have all nations rally to him is Jesus Christ. No other historical figure tracing his lineage back to Jesse can make that claim. This is particularly fitting for the only innocent man to allow himself to be crucified for our sins on a tree and **"stand as a banner for the peoples."**

What is a banner? A banner is a sign, symbol or message designed to draw people to a nation, leader, or other cause. Does that not fit the cross completely? We must be drawn to the banner of the cross every day. Jesus' **"place of rest"** was indeed **"glorious"** because he rose from the dead! Think about Jesus' resurrection; is there anything else more worthy of drawing us in? Certainly not. Don't fight God. Allow yourself to be drawn into the amazing message of the cross.

This chapter of Isaiah closes with a hopeful prophecy about **"the remnant"** of God's people. We are promised **"a highway"** as good as the one that led the Israelites out of Egypt!

Isaiah 11:16 **"There will be a highway for the remnant of his people that is left from Assyria, as there was for Israel when they came up from Egypt."**

Isn't it exciting to know that the highway God has prepared for us today is as miraculous as the parting of the Red Sea? That path is the narrow road that Jesus marks out for his faithful followers. In Isaiah 35:8-9, this same highway is called **"the Way of Holiness,"** a road in which **"only the redeemed will walk there."** Isaiah is talking about the spiritual road paved with the cross, the resurrection, and the promise of being born again **"of water and the Spirit"** (John 3:1-7). Let's take that route: no more dead-end roads. Get on the holy highway!

The Branch is also a clear prophecy describing Jesus a number of times in Jeremiah. We will look at one in great detail, because it shows Jesus as both man and God!

Jeremiah 23:5-6 **"'The days are coming,' declares the LORD, 'when I will raise up to David a righteous Branch, a King who will reign wisely and do what is just and right in the land. In his days Judah will be saved and Israel will live in safety. This is the name by which he will be called: The LORD Our Righteousness.'"**

In no uncertain terms, this is saying that the Branch will be David's descendent, a wise and just king, and this king is also known as **"The LORD Our Righteousness."** In other words, a future king from David's line will be more than a great ruler--he will be God, and he will save his people. As with all messianic prophecy, this is exactly true about Jesus, and only true about Jesus.

The people who scoff at the concept of God becoming a man simply don't know the Scriptures or the power of God. Why couldn't God become a man? Is he not powerful or smart enough to figure out how to do that? If only those who claim respect for God's word would actually read it with an open mind, they would see that the entire Bible--Old and New Testaments--are full of clear statements that can point only to Jesus being God.

Memorize the fact that one of Jesus' messianic names is **"The LORD Our Righteousness."** This is an accurate prediction that the only way anyone can be righteous is through Jesus. He is **"Our Righteousness."** We can't be righteous (doing what is right in the eyes of God) by our own abilities. We need Jesus' cleansing from sin and his Holy Spirit to be **"Our"** guide to righteousness.

Do not think that you can do things by your own power or your own righteousness. That will not last for long. In fact, it will fail. I know this from firsthand experience. The only way to "live in safety" is to trust in Jesus' righteousness. Trust in him. Through Jesus is the only way to be saved.

Ten chapters later, Jeremiah mentions the Branch again (Jeremiah 33:15-16). The verses are nearly identical. Thereafter, a remarkable prophecy about the priesthood is foretold.

Jeremiah 33:17-18, 22 **"For this is what the LORD says: 'David will never fail to have a man to sit on the throne of the house of Israel, nor will the priests, who are Levites, ever fail to have a man to stand before me continually to offer burnt offerings, to burn grain offerings and to present sacrifices.... I will make the descendants of David my servant and the Levites who minister before me as countless as the stars of the sky and as measureless as the sand on the seashore.'"**

Here is the promise that, when the Branch comes (Jesus), he will create a kingdom of his priests who are **"as countless as the stars of the sky."** In other words, here is an accurate prediction that, under the New Covenant, every true disciple of Jesus will be a priest.

1 Peter 2:9 confirms this. **"But you are a chosen people, a royal priesthood, a holy nation, a people belonging to God...."**

All God's people are part of a royal priesthood with Jesus, the descendent of David, ruling on the throne. If you are a Christian, do you take your role as a priest seriously? Is it a lifestyle, or just a Sunday game-face? When Peter says the disciples are a **"holy nation,"** I'm sure he was referring to every day. So to my fellow priests, I say let's live every day as set aside and holy to the Lord!

Continuing our study of Zechariah, you should be able to find many more beacons pointing to Jesus throughout the whole book. Some of the most vivid of these prophecies come in the later portion of Zechariah.

Zechariah 11:10 **"Then I took my staff called Favor and broke it, revoking the covenant I had made with all the nations."**

Here is God prophesying about how he will revoke (as in put an end to) the Old Covenant. This, of course, soon paves the way for the New Covenant. But first a price is paid to get out of the old agreement with God.

Zechariah 11:12-13 **"I told them, 'If you think it best, give me my pay; but if not, keep it.' So they paid me thirty pieces of silver. And the LORD said to me, 'Throw it to the potter'--the handsome price at which they priced me! So I took the thirty pieces of silver and threw them into the house of the LORD to the potter.'"**

Thirty pieces of silver is the price associated with breaking the Old Covenant. The LORD says that thirty silver pieces is the **"price at which they priced me!"** This is saying that God's people only valued God at thirty silver pieces. To appreciate the significance of this, we need to look at the details surrounding Judas' betrayal of Jesus. The questions to keep in mind here are why was the money thrown into the temple, and how does **"the potter"** fit into all this?

Matthew 26:14-15 **"Then one of the Twelve--the one called Judas Iscariot--went to the chief priests and asked, 'What are you willing to give me if I hand him over to you?' So they counted out for him thirty silver coins."**

We can see from Zechariah and Matthew, that the price of betrayal is identical: thirty silver coins. As in Zechariah, God (as Jesus) is only valued at thirty silver coins. Incidentally, for our own development, we must ask ourselves a similar question; how much do we value God? Does it show in our lives? Is it evident in how we spend our time and money? If we understand that we are a part of the predicted betrayal of Jesus--that we are also responsible for his death--then we should also show our gratitude by living lives that honor God.

So far, Zechariah's prophecy is parallel to Jesus being betrayed and Judas' demise. But Zechariah also mentions a potter and that the silver was thrown into the house of the LORD. This is fulfilled one chapter later in Matthew.

Matthew 27:3-10 **"When Judas, who had betrayed him, saw that Jesus was condemned, he was seized with remorse and returned the thirty silver coins to the chief priests and the elders. 'I have sinned,' he said, 'for I have betrayed innocent blood.' 'What is that to us?' they replied. 'That's your responsibility.' So Judas threw the money into the temple and left. Then he went away and hanged himself. The chief priests picked up the coins and said, 'It is against the law to put this into the treasury, since it is blood money.' So they decided to use the money to buy the potter's field as a burial place for foreigners. That is why it has been called the Field of Blood to this day. Then what was spoken by Jeremiah the prophet was fulfilled: 'They took the thirty silver coins, the price set on him by the people of Israel, and they used them to buy the potter's field, as the Lord commanded me.'"**

We see here that Zechariah's prophecy completely comes true through Judas' act of betrayal. In both cases, the thirty silver coins were thrown into God's temple. In both cases, the money doesn't stay in the temple. It ends up going to the potter as the purchase price for a place to bury foreigners. Jeremiah is also quoted as prophesying about this incident, and to study that out, you can see Jeremiah 19:1-13 and Jeremiah 32:6-9.

Zechariah 12:7 **"The LORD will save the dwellings of Judah first..."**

Jesus, as the descendant and lion of Judah (Genesis 49:8-10), will be the first person resurrected (saved after death) into the New Covenant. The name "Judah" means "praise" (see Genesis 29:35), which is a fitting name that foreshadows the coming of Jesus, who deserves all of our praise.

Saving **"the dwellings of Judah first"** has an added meaning for anyone following (or dwelling in) Jesus. If your commitment, hope, faith, love, and obedience lies in Jesus, you too will dwell with him and be saved!

Zechariah 12:10 **"And I will pour out on the house of David and the inhabitants of Jerusalem a spirit of grace and supplication. They will look on me, the one they have pierced, and they will mourn for him as one mourns for an only child, and grieve bitterly for him as one grieves for a firstborn son."**

The LORD God says that he will be **"pierced"** by his own people and then they will "mourn for him" as an only child and grieve for him as **"a firstborn son."** How in the world could God be pierced? Only by becoming a man for our benefit (grace/favor). That's Jesus Christ.

This piercing is described as an act of **"grace and supplication"** through the house of David. God is basically saying that Jesus' crucifixion was an act of grace (favor) and brought about supplication for his people. Supplication means "humble prayer," so God uses the cross to help us be humble, see our need for God, and pray to him out of gratitude and reverence.

The prophecy assumes that Jesus won't stay dead, because the verses after this one describe the many things God will still be doing.

Zechariah 13:1 **"On that day a fountain will be opened to the house of David and the inhabitants of Jerusalem, to cleanse them from sin and impurity."**

God promises that the outcome of the cross is that his people have the opportunity to get their sins forgiven--to be clean!

Zechariah 13:2 **"'On that day, I will banish the names of the idols from the land, and they will be remembered no more,' declares the LORD Almighty. 'I will remove both the prophets and the spirit of impurity from the land.'"**

God goes on to proclaim his victory over idols. We can be free from the false gods of idolatry; we just need Jesus. Forget the idols in your life.

107

God says here that he will also remove the prophets after this period. In other words, after the New Testament writers completed the Bible (which recorded the cross, resurrection and Jesus' first century church), there would be no more need for prophets. This verse alone refutes Muslims, Mormons, Jehovah's Witnesses, and any other false religious groups who take later man-made teachings and try to pass them off as further prophecies. Look at Zechariah 13:2 carefully; the LORD Almighty says that he will **"remove"** the prophets from the land.

Jesus knows how to "clean house." Removing the false prophets and the **"spirit of impurity from the land"** shows Jesus' commitment to have a pure relationship with those who appreciate his amazing sacrifice. Why would God go through all this trouble? Jesus wants an uncomplicated, unhindered close relationship with you through the cross. God does his part. Let's do our part by living a life of purity and gratitude at the foot of the cross and before the empty tomb!

Chapter 15: Rebuilding and Reforming under Zerubbabel

Not a whole lot is known about the Old Testament leader named Zerubbabel. Most people couldn't even tell you a thing about him. Nevertheless, he is an extremely important figure whom, the more you know about him, the more you get excited about the Messiah. First and foremost, Zerubbabel is in the direct family line of Jesus. He is an ancestor of Joseph, who was a father to Jesus.

Matthew 1:12, 16 **"After the exile to Babylon: Jeconiah was the father of Shealtiel, Shealtiel the father of Zerubbabel... and Jacob the father of Joseph, the husband of Mary, of whom was born Jesus, who is called Christ."**

Of course, reading the entire lineage listed in Matthew 1, you might easily conclude that a lot of people were in the family line of Jesus. They can't all be amazing people. That is true, but Zerubbabel deserves a deeper look, because what God does with him is amazing.

The first mention of Zerubbabel in the Bible is in 1 Chronicles 3:17-19. There it is recorded that Zerubbabel is a great-grandson of King Jehoiachin, the exiled ruler of Judah who was brought into Babylonian captivity. In fact, the name Zerubbabel means "sown in Babylon," or "born at Babylon." We shall look at a number of parallels between Zerubbabel and Jesus. Both men led their people out of captivity, and these parallels are so amazing, that they're messianic.

Ezra 3:2-3 **"Then Jeshua son of Jozadak and his fellow priests and Zerubbabel son of Shealtiel and his associates began to build the altar of the God of Israel to sacrifice burnt offerings on it, in accordance with what is written in the Law of Moses the man of God. Despite their fear of the peoples around them, they built the altar on its foundation and sacrificed burnt offerings on it to the LORD, both the morning and evening sacrifices."**

Zerubbabel is one of the men who leads God's people out of their 70 years of Babylonian captivity. In Ezra we find that he is a reformer and doesn't cave in to fear. He does what is right and (along with the other leaders) rebuilds the altar of God and restores their practice of making appropriate sacrifices to God. This is like Jesus, a reformer who didn't give in to **"fear of the peoples around"** him. Both men restored people to God. Of course Jesus didn't merely offer animal sacrifices to God--he became the atoning (wrath-removing) sacrifice for our sins. That's the ultimate sacrifice.

Ezra 3:8 "In the second month of the second year after their arrival at the house of God in Jerusalem, Zerubbabel son of Shealtiel, Jeshua son of Jozadak and the rest of their brothers (the priests and the Levites and all who had returned from the captivity to Jerusalem) began the work, appointing Levites twenty years of age and older to supervise the building of the house of the LORD."

Zerubbabel is one of the courageous men who leads the rebuilding **"of the house of the LORD."** This is a key role of the Messiah. How does the rebuilding get done? Zerubbbel (and the other leaders) began **"appointing Levites"** to **"supervise the building of the house of the LORD."** We see that appointing appropriate people is how the job gets done. Zerubbabel works through people, as does Jesus, who appointed his disciples (Luke 10:1). Jesus rebuilt the New Testament house of God as a totally committed assembly of believers whom he had appointed. That's the church--the household of God, as described in its fulfilment in Ephesians 2.

Ephesians 2:19-22 **"Consequently, you are no longer foreigners and aliens, but fellow citizens with God's people and members of God's household, built on the foundation of the apostles and prophets, with Christ Jesus himself as the chief cornerstone. In him the whole building is joined together and rises to become a holy temple in the Lord. And in him you too are being built together to become a dwelling in which God lives by his Spirit."**

The house of the LORD--God's holy temple--is not merely built by faithful people: it is composed of faithful people. God's people are the bricks, with Jesus the Messiah as the **"chief cornerstone."** Jesus is not just the cornerstone; he is also the bonding agent who holds his disciples (the temple) together by his Holy Spirit. The Holy Spirit is not merely the glue, an inert object holding people together. Rather the assembly of Jesus' disciples becomes **"a dwelling in which God lives by his Spirit."** That's what true church is: not a physical building, but a rebuilt family of the faithful, wherein God himself **"lives."**

It took faith for Zerubbabel to rebuild God's temple despite local opposition, and it took faith for Jesus to rebuild God's temple as his church in the New Testament--despite much opposition. Yet Zerubbabel, as a messianic figure, and Jesus, as the Messiah, got the job done!

We also see in in Zerubbabel's time that the rebuilding of the temple is a sign of God's everlasting love.

Ezra 3:10-11 **"When the builders laid the foundation of the temple of the LORD... with praise and thanksgiving they sang to the LORD: 'He is good; his love to Israel endures forever.'"**

Indeed, God's love does endure forever through the church. As a unified assembly of evangelistic believers, the true church members are the ones who bring the message of God's unending love to the lost people of today. Thus the building process of God's holy temple continues as more disciples **"make disciples of all nations,"** which is what we are commanded to do (Matthew 28:19-20) by Jesus.

In Ezra we also see a controversial role of the Messiah: to keep false worshipers out of God's holy temple.

Ezra 4:1-4 **"When the enemies of Judah and Benjamin heard that the exiles were building a temple for the LORD, the God of Israel, they came to Zerubbabel and to the heads of the families and said, 'Let us help you build because, like you, we seek your God and have been sacrificing to him since the time of Esarhaddon king of Assyria, who brought us here.' But Zerubbabel, Jeshua and the rest of the heads of the families of Israel answered, 'You have no part with us in building a temple to our God. We alone will build it for the LORD, the God of Israel, as King Cyrus, the king of Persia, commanded us.' Then the peoples around them set out to discourage the people of Judah and make them afraid to go on building."**

Political correctness is completely out the window here. The help of insincere religious people is completely rejected. This is a sobering reminder that not everyone who claims to **"seek"** God actually makes it to a relationship with God. The issue here is that the people who weren't allowed to help build the temple weren't really seeking God with all of their hearts. And that is a must (Jeremiah 29:11-14)! Therefore people who aren't totally committed were excluded from the assembly of God. We see that this is the case in the Old Testament here, and also the case in the New Testament.

Luke 14:33 **"In the same way, any of you who does not give up everything he has cannot be my disciple."**

We see that casual helpers are not called to be Jesus' disciples. In fact, Jesus says that people who hold back in their commitment **"cannot be my disciple."** Only totally committed followers--those who have given up everything--are eligible to be part of God's holy temple: the church.

You may say that you're no enemy of God, and it is hard to relate to the troublemakers in Ezra 4 who tried to stop the work on God's temple. But look at your own life. What have you been appointed to do and are you doing it? Are you building for God? Who has appointed you? Is this process biblical, or a made up tradition of men.

Also ask yourself about what you are really building? Will it last? Would God be pleased with it? What is your part in the work? How is your own sincerity toward God? We see from Ezra 4 that not everyone gets to take part in rebuilding God's temple. Some sacrifices are simply not acceptable, and people can be deceived about how to be included as a true member of Jesus' church.

So **"watch your life and doctrine closely"** (1 Timothy 4:16), and embrace the role that God has assigned for you to do. Anything less is rebellion against God. One of the reasons Zerubbabel is highly regarded in the Bible is that he embraced his role and he kept good company.

Nehemiah 7:6-7 **"These are the people of the province who came up from the captivity of the exiles whom Nebuchadnezzar king of Babylon had taken captive (they returned to Jerusalem and Judah, each to his own town, in company with Zerubbabel, Jeshua, Nehemiah, Azariah, Raamiah, Nahamani, Mordecai, Bilshan, Mispereth, Bigvai, Nehum and Baanah):"**

This list of leaders with Zerubbabel is impressive. Nehemiah is mentioned as well as Mordecai, the main male leader of God's people from the book of Esther. This reminds me of Proverbs 13:20.

"He who walks with the wise grows wise, but a companion of fools suffers harm." I get the sense that these were hard times that God used to forge faithful men into godly leaders, and they learned from each other. Also take a count of the number of leaders named here. There are 12, which may be a foreshadowing of Jesus' 12 apostles.

In Nehemiah 12 (entire chapter), we also learn that Zerubbabel was also with Ezra the priest and scribe, Zechariah the prophet/priest, and many other godly men. This is an all-star cast of faithful leaders whom God has assembled around Zerubbabel in a time of great restoration. Is this not what Jesus does--restoring souls while assembling and forging the future leaders? In the case of Jesus, he is still doing it today and you are invited to be a part of it!

Studying the life of Zerubbabel, it becomes clear that God was constantly refining him into the leader he was meant to be. As governor of Judah (Haggai 1:1), Zerubbabel and Joshua are admonished by God through the prophet Haggai to build God's house and not their own **"paneled houses."** The result is that Zerubbabel and Joshua obey and God is with them. Moreover, "the LORD stirred up the spirit of Zerubbabel" along with the spirit of all the people, and God's temple starts getting rebuilt (Haggai 1:12-14).

A great (yet simple) lesson can be gleaned from this: God leads, leaders follow God, and then the people follow God too. Whole nations benefit as a result. For your own personal growth, make sure you are part of this plan too. Many people, when asked, would say that they are following God directly. However, when those same people are asked if they follow godly leaders, you get a lot of blank stares. That's because people are independent and in their pride, they don't really want to be led. But we see here (and throughout the Bible) that people following God through godly leaders is part of the plan.

Haggai 2:4-5 **"'But now be strong, O Zerubbabel,' declares the LORD. 'Be strong, O Joshua son of Jehozadak, the high priest. Be strong, all you people of the land,' declares the LORD, 'and work. For I am with you,' declares the LORD Almighty. 'This is what I covenanted with you when you came out of Egypt. And my Spirit remains among you. Do not fear.'"**

Foreshadowed in the book of Haggai also is the dual role of the Messiah as high priest and ruler. The Messiah is represented symbolically by Joshua and Zerubbabel. In fact, what is said to these Old Testament leaders applies to Jesus as well as these leaders. Jesus was strengthened by the LORD Almighty. Jesus worked because the LORD was with him. The LORD's Spirit remains among Jesus.

As is common with messianic prophecy that is true about Jesus as well as an Old Testament figure, there often comes a turning point in such prophecies. Information shifts from having dual truths about an Old Testament figure plus Jesus to information that can only be true about Jesus. See the verse below from Haggai and see if you can spot the turning point where the prophecy breaks out of Old Testament symbolism and becomes exclusive only to Jesus.

Haggai 2:7-9 **"'I will shake all nations, and the desired of all nations will come, and I will fill this house with glory,' says the LORD Almighty. 'The silver is mine and the gold is mine,' declares the LORD Almighty. 'The glory of this present house will be greater than the glory of the former house,' says the LORD Almighty. 'And in this place I will grant peace,' declares the LORD Almighty."**

The practical application of God filling **"this house with glory"** refers to the second temple being built after end of the Babylonian exile. Meanwhile, the New Testament application refers to the establishment of Jesus' church, which continues to **"shake all nations."** Then did you catch the exclusive breakout point in the prophecy: the point that can only refer to Jesus? It begins with **"The glory of this present house will be greater than the glory of the former house."** God is talking about the church, because the members will have the indwelling of Jesus' Holy Spirit and in this way, God **"will grant them peace."**

Haggai chapter 2 closes with a prophecy that is really all about, and only about Jesus.

Haggai 2:21-23 **"'Tell Zerubbabel governor of Judah that I will shake the heavens and the earth. I will overturn royal thrones and shatter the power of the foreign kingdoms. I will overthrow chariots and their drivers; horses and their riders will fall, each by the sword of his brother. 'On that day,' declares the**

LORD Almighty, 'I will take you, my servant Zerubbabel son of Shealtiel,' declares the LORD, 'and I will make you like my signet ring, for I have chosen you,' declares the LORD Almighty."**

We know that the above verse can't really be about the leaders mentioned in this verse because Israel never became a world power under Zerubbabel. After the Persians ruled over them, they were dominated by the Greeks and then the Romans. But under Jesus, the mighty Messiah, God's spiritual kingdom--the church--has become the chosen place of God's new dwelling.

Moreover, it is Jesus, the very word of God (John 1), who is like God's **"signet ring."** An extension of a ruler's power and sign of personal approval, the signet ring metaphor is God's way of saying that Jesus has his full and personal approval. In other words, if it came from Jesus, then it came from God. Jesus confirms this throughout his ministry.

John 14:10 **"Don't you believe that I am in the Father, and that the Father is in me? The words I say to you are not just my own. Rather, it is the Father, living in me, who is doing his work."**

Jesus' every word has the stamp of God's signet ring. Through the messianic representation of Zerubbabel, God has given us more proof that the Messiah will be the **"chosen"** representation of God on earth, and this will be glorious.

Despite Zerubbabel's absence from modern-day discussion, we have seen that he actually appears many more times than most people might think in the Bible--in both Old and New Testaments. In total, 1st Chronicles, Ezra, Nehemiah, Haggai, Zechariah, Matthew and Luke mention Zerubbabel by name and usually with significant messianic application. That's because Zerubbabel is one of the key men in all of history who are highly symbolic of amazing things to come.

Men Symbolic of Things to Come

Throughout the Bible, many men are **"men symbolic of things to come."** In the book of Zechariah, both Joshua, the high priest, and

Zerubbabel, the governor, are remarkable men holding two different offices who become messianic symbols of Jesus.

Zechariah 3:8 **"Listen, O high priest Joshua and your associates seated before you, who are men symbolic of things to come..."**

In Zechariah 3:8, the symbolic associates of Joshua noted in Zechariah 3 are not mentioned by name. However, one chapter later, Zerubbabel is discussed in fantastic, prophetic, and symbolic detail. Therefore it is natural to conclude that Zerubbabel is one of Joshua's seated associates **"who are men symbolic of things to come."** Indeed, Zechariah 4 displays the mighty messianic nature of Zerubbabel.

Zechariah 4

1 "Then the angel who talked with me returned and wakened me, as a man is wakened from his sleep.

2 He asked me, 'What do you see?' I answered, 'I see a solid gold lampstand with a bowl at the top and seven lights on it, with seven channels to the lights.

3 Also there are two olive trees by it, one on the right of the bowl and the other on its left.'

4 I asked the angel who talked with me, 'What are these, my lord?'

5 He answered, 'Do you not know what these are?' 'No, my lord,' I replied.

6 So he said to me, 'This is the word of the LORD to Zerubbabel: "Not by might nor by power, but by my Spirit," says the LORD Almighty.

7 'What are you, O mighty mountain? Before Zerubbabel you will become level ground. Then he will bring out the capstone to shouts of "God bless it! God bless it!"

8 Then the word of the LORD came to me:

9 'The hands of Zerubbabel have laid the foundation of this temple; his hands will also complete it. Then you will know that the LORD Almighty has sent me to you.

10 Who despises the day of small things? Men will rejoice when they see the plumb line in the hand of Zerubbabel. (These

seven are the eyes of the LORD, which range throughout the earth.)'

11 **Then I asked the angel, 'What are these two olive trees on the right and the left of the lampstand?'**

12 **Again I asked him, 'What are these two olive branches beside the two gold pipes that pour out golden oil?'**

13 **He replied, 'Do you not know what these are?' 'No, my lord,' I said.**

14 **So he said, 'These are the two who are anointed to serve the Lord of all the earth.'"**

There's a lot of symbolism to absorb here from Zechariah 4, some of which we may not fully understand until God reveals it to his people in paradise. Yet what can we get right now from this chapter? Quite a bit:

Verses 2-3: God's word and his church are **"solid gold,"** as in highly valued, pure, and radiant. God's kingdom is also full of perfect light, represented by the golden lampstand with seven lights.

Verse 4: The two olive trees represent the never ending light of God that is Jesus Christ. Light for the lamp comes specifically from olive oil (Exodus 25:6). That the church is surrounded on both sides by an abundant light source shows how God will not run out of fuel to get the job done. On the cross, Jesus appeared to run out of light/fuel because he died. But three days later, he rose! Therefore Jesus has all the resources to start the church and finish the work of the church. These two olive trees also represent the anointing of God. Anointing oil comes from olive trees (Exodus 30:22-33). We need to seek God's anointing--his covering and blessing in a spiritual sense.

As if these two olive oil references (light and anointing) were not enough, there is much more to understand about the significance of the olive tree. The manna from heaven that the Israelites ate as food from God **"tasted like something made with olive oil"** (Numbers 11:7-8). Also in Genesis 8:11, the first sign that Noah had about the flood finally being over was when the dove returned to Noah with **"a freshly plucked olive leaf."** In 1 Kings 6:23, the cherubim in the inner sanctuary are made of olive wood 15 feet high. In 1 Kings 6:31, the doors to the inner sanctuary are made of olive wood. In

John 18:1, we discover that the garden of Gethsemane, where Jesus was arrested, was an **"olive grove."** In Romans 11:17-24, the church is described as an olive tree. It's as if God really wants his people to understand something supernaturally special about olive trees: when you think of olive tree and its fruit, you think of God!

Let's get back to the detailed analysis of Zechariah 4.

Verse 6: The church gets built by God's Spirit. As an invisible holy agent, God is getting things done. He certainly has **"power,"** but he gets the job done by his unseen Spirit. Right before he died, Jesus said, **"Father, into your hands I commit my spirit"** (Luke 23:46). With Zechariah 4:6 prophesying **"Not by might nor by power, but by my Spirit,"** it predicts that the establishment of God's kingdom is built on Jesus laying down his spirit at the cross.

The word **"might"** used here is translated from the Hebrew word "chayil." It means "strength, power, might (especially warlike), valor" (Source: Genenius' Hebrew-Chaldee Lexicon). God certainly has immeasurable **"might,"** but he doesn't start a physical war to pave the way for the church. Instead he has Jesus show his trust in the Father by laying down his spirit. Then after the resurrection, which was enabled by God's Spirit, the church begins with its founding moment from Acts 2:38-41, where 3,000 people accept the command to **"repent and be baptized."** What's the Holy Spirit doing here? Among other things, he dwells inside the new members of the church, making them holy. From Zechariah 4:6, we see that indeed, **"By [God's] Spirit"** is how the church gets founded and built. Think also about how God decides to foreshadow this event prophetically. He chooses Zerubbabel as the man symbolic of Jesus, the spiritual builder of the church. That is quite an honor.

Verse 7: The Messiah, symbolized here by Zerubbabel and the capstone, will level the other kingdoms (**"mountains"**). These other **"mountains"** (kingdoms) will all become **"level ground"** before Jesus and his church.

Verse 10: Be glad and **"rejoice"** that Jesus has measured out (with **"the plumb line"**) how the church will operate and who will be in it. Indeed, people saw the full measure of God's love through Jesus' literal **"hand"** while he was crucified (hands and feet) to the

118

cross. The punishment measured out for us was reassigned to the hands of the Messiah.

Also in verse 10, we see that the seven lights from the lampstand are **"the eyes of the LORD, which range throughout the earth."** So God sees everything and he is particularly interested in viewing our lives. God cares! He's not some local "god" who is aloofly engaged in random and vague activity. He is the one true God over all, and his message lights up those around the world who obey it.

Verses 11-14: That there are two olive trees/branches refers to the two anointed offices of God: priest and king. Jesus, the anointed son of God, holds both offices: priest and king. This priest-king is **"anointed to serve the Lord of all the earth."** Doing God's will on earth through amazing acts of service is what Jesus does throughout his entire ministry.

No one served God like Jesus. In the entire history of the human race, no one even comes close. Therefore, we need to be in awe of Jesus' respect and service to the Father, who gets things done by the unseen anointing through his Holy Spirit. Moreover, we need imitate Jesus by giving great respect and service to God.

Revelation 11 confirms that the two anointed men referenced in Zechariah 4:14 are prophets, witnesses, and that they are active for about three and a half years, then they die, but three days later, they rise again. Written in apocalyptic language, these two men are really Jesus as two manifestations of God: God the Son, and God the Holy Spirit. Let's break it down.

Revelation 11:3-4 **"And I will give power to my two witnesses, and they will prophesy for 1,260 days, clothed in sackcloth. These are the two olive trees and the two lampstands that stand before the Lord of the earth."**

It is well known that Jesus preached for just over three years (1,260 days). See how Revelation ties the two witnesses with that three-year mission? These two prophets, which are really two manifestations of the Messiah (Jesus and the Holy Spirit), are also symbolic of the two olive trees and lampstands **"that stand before the Lord of all the earth."** In fact, if you blend the vision in Zechariah 4 with its counterpart in Revelation 11, you get two olive trees plus one lampstand in the middle. These three forms help us comprehend the triune nature of God. It's as if God knows we need many examples to comprehend him, and he is expanding our understanding of the Trinity by displaying these three forms in the vision.

Revelation 11:7-9 **"Now when they have finished their testimony, the beast that comes up from the Abyss will attack them, and overpower and kill them. Their bodies will lie in the street of the great city, which is figuratively called Sodom and Egypt, where also their Lord was crucified. For three and a half days men from every people, tribe, language and nation will gaze on their bodies and refuse them burial."**

Here we have an apocalyptic depiction of Jesus' death. A three day period in Jerusalem is described, because that's how long Jesus was dead for: three days. Don't be thrown off by the phrase about people gazing at the bodies and them being refused a burial. Think about Jesus' death and burial: it wasn't the usual kind; people did gaze at Jesus' body on the cross for many hours. Also, at the burial, Jesus was refused a typical burial in that Roman guards were stationed at his tomb for three days.

Revelation 11:11 **"But after the three and a half days a breath of life from God entered them, and they stood on their feet, and terror struck those who saw them."**

Does this not describe the resurrection? Jesus dies, but **"after the three and a half days a breath of life from God entered them...."** God raised Jesus to life again. Jesus is described as **"them"** because the Holy Spirit returned to his body. With the Holy Spirit, Jesus (Also known here as **"them"**) rose after three days and the Roman soldiers were terrified because of it. The details fit with alarming clarity.

Matthew 28:1-6 **"...Mary Magdalene and the other Mary went to look at the tomb. There was a violent earthquake, for an angel of the Lord came down from heaven and, going to the tomb, rolled back the stone and sat on it. His appearance was like lightning, and his clothes were white as snow. The guards were so afraid of him that they shook and became like dead men. The angel said to the women, 'Do not be afraid, for I know that** you are looking for Jesus, who was crucified. He is not here; he has risen, just as he said. Come and see the place where he lay.'"

For even more proof that Revelation is all about the victory of the cross and the resurrection of Christ (as opposed to some futuristic sci-fi plot as some have made the book out to be), even the **"violent earthquake"** that Matthew 28 mentions at the resurrection of Jesus is also described in Revelation, just a few verses after Jesus' third-day resurrection is stated.

Revelation 11:12-13 **"Then they heard a loud voice from heaven saying to them, 'Come up here.' And they went up to heaven in a cloud, while their enemies looked on. At that very hour there was a severe earthquake and a tenth of the city collapsed. Seven thousand people were killed in the earthquake, and the survivors were terrified and gave glory to the God of heaven."**

Contrary to a popular belief that everyone who claims Christ is a Christian, we see from Revelation 11 that while Jesus was being resurrected, many others were dying! In other words, only the faithful look forward to the resurrection. If your heart is beating today, then you may be one of **"the survivors,"** but are you one of the faithful? If so, it is time to get a holy fear of God and bow down before Jesus Christ, who rose from the dead on the third day and went up to heaven in a cloud.

Stop trying to build up your city, which will **"collapse"** eventually. Rather now is the time to build up Jesus' kingdom on earth--the church. Let's give **"glory to the God of heaven"** by obeying and worshiping him as the mighty Messiah that Jesus was, is, and always will be!

Chapter 16: What about People Who Never Heard of Jesus?

It is important to acknowledge that there are many people today who have no idea *what* a messiah is let alone *who* the Messiah is. While Jesus is the Messiah--the anointed, chosen redeemer and God in the flesh--some entire countries are taught from birth that there is no God. Other peoples are taught with great intensity about a false god or gods through traditions that have been handed down for generations.

Therefore the following question comes up often enough: With billions of people in the world from countless religions, is there really only one way to be saved--through Jesus the Messiah? The short answer is "Yes, because the Bible says so." For those who really trust God, the short answer should be enough. The Bible says it, and that settles it.

Zechariah 14:9 **"The LORD will be king over the whole earth. On that day there will be one LORD, and his name the only name."**

The Old Testament confirms that there is only **"one LORD, and his name the only name."** This is a prophecy about the Messiah: the master, the king, and the only God. In the New Testament, Peter refers to Jesus by name to specify the only name by which we must be saved:

Acts 4:10, 12 **"It is by the name of Jesus Christ... Salvation is found in no one else, for there is no other name under heaven given to men by which we must be saved."**

Putting just these two verses together we can conclude with brevity that Jesus is God, he's the only God, and he's the only way for all people to be saved. That's the short answer to the question "What about people who never heard of Jesus?" They need to hear about Jesus and follow him; their salvation depends on it!

Thankfully, God is patient with us. For those who have yet to fully put their trust in God, there is, of course, a longer answer as well. As for brevity, it is out the window.

The Long Answer to the Question about the Fate of Non-Christians

As a non-believer many years ago, I had asked what I felt was a very essential question to a young woman who had recently become a Christian. I said to her, "What about people who believe in some other god? Like what about Buddhists in Asia who have never even heard of Jesus Christ? Are you trying to tell me that they are going to hell just because they don't know Jesus?"

I thought for sure I had trapped her with my brilliant question. She couldn't possibly answer it well because we both knew that she didn't know anybody in Asia. Nevertheless, this new Christian looked right through me with an uncanny confidence and replied, "Look here; Buddha didn't die for anybody's sin. But Jesus was crucified for your sake. He died for your sin. Now as for people in Asia, I don't know them. But if I did meet them, I would tell them the same thing: that Jesus died for their sin too, and the only way to get to heaven is through Jesus Christ. But I'm not talking to them now; I'm talking to you! You need to seek God with all your heart. Your very life depends on it!"

That conversation stirred my soul like never before. Consequentially, a few months later (long story, short), after deeper Bible study, I ended up doing something I had never imagined doing:

1) I believed.
2) I made Jesus the Lord (master) of my life.
3) I became cut to the heart over my sin.
4) I repented of my sin.
5) I got baptized.

As a former doubter/antagonist/rebel against God, I had finally become a Christian. The icing on the cake is that this young woman later became my wife. Now, as members of the church, we live by this conviction: that Jesus is **"the way and the truth and the life. No one comes to the Father except through"** him (John 14:6).

The truth of my beliefs aside, day after day around the world there are still people asking those same questions; what about people who never heard of Jesus or the gospel? It is such a common thought that I'm asked that very question frequently. There is something universal to each of these conversations. Strangers, friends, family members, and even fellow Christians have this question on their hearts. Do you know how to answer?

The exact phrase "what about people who never heard of Jesus" shows up on at least 31,000 different web pages according to Google as well as Microsoft (Bing) searches. That represents a lot of people asking and trying to answer that vital question of faith. If not properly addressed, the question of what happens to people who don't know about the Messiah and never heard the gospel could easily fester into a doorway for doubt and indecision. Such unsettling doubt may reign in the lives of non-believers and believers alike, making their lives unfruitful.

If Christians are right about only Christians being saved, then the stakes are as high as heaven (salvation) for the Christians and as low as the grave and hell (torment) for those who reject Jesus. But if Christians are wrong, and a person can get to heaven without Jesus, then Christians are living a lie. Appropriately answering the question, "What about people who don't know about Jesus?" is essential to the Christian faith. It influences our urgency to reach out to the lost and it forces us to look very closely at Jesus' words and ask, "Do we really believe? Can one Messiah really cover the whole world? Is Jesus really Lord of all?"

Thankfully, God has created a simple authentication process, built right into the Bible and it is meant to answer questions, but only for people taking action. In John 7:17, Jesus explains, **"If anyone chooses to do God's will, he will find out whether my teaching comes from God or whether I speak on my own."**

This is a promise from Jesus. The uncertain people can **"find out"** if the Bible is from God simply by doing what Jesus teaches. Living out what Jesus says to do can build a person's faith in God. I experienced this quickly after only a day or so of studying the Bible. I stopped swearing for a whole day and immediately noticed that my mind was clearer and cleaner in my thoughts--even less bitter. I recognized this as internal proof that what Jesus says to do is from God.

The Global Importance of Jesus

Thankfully, the Bible gives us an inspiring picture of all that God is doing to address the manmade confusion around those who have never heard of Jesus. One of the first big concepts about God to keep in mind (and it should give us all comfort) is that God is a just judge. He is not going to be improperly assessing you or your ancestors. Psalm 96:13 states that the LORD **"...comes to judge the earth. He will judge the world in righteousness and the peoples in his truth."** God has all of the information to make the right judgments about all of our lives, not according to our limited perception of truth, but according to **"his truth."** Keep in mind that this is judgment of **"the earth"** and **"the world."** That means judgment on an international/global scale.

So many people have a hard time trusting God because they trust their own fragmented view of what they *think* is truth over God's global, comprehensive, and objective view of truth. That's pride, elevating your own view over God's way. Pride will stop people from seeing God's truth. For most people stuck in their own incorrect view of truth, it would be essential to do a study on pride. Proverbs 16:25 sums up the folly of pride; **"There is a way that seems right to a man, but in the end it leads to death."** Other helpful Scriptures on pride include Isaiah 30:1-22, Job 21:14-15, 1 Samuel 15:1-35, and Proverbs 3:5. Individuals need to push past their pride; they need to see the folly of their own arrogant logic and in humility, start trusting in God's ability to make the best and completely appropriate judgment in all matters, in all time periods, and for all nations.

As written in Psalm 96:10, **"...he will judge the peoples with equity."** In other words, when God makes his judgments, the actions of all peoples in all nations are taken into account. There is equity: equal treatment, even for obscure nations that we may never know ourselves. But God knows them: he creates and sustains them. He knows their every thought, conversation, action, and opportunity.

Evidence of God is available to those obscure nations as well. Psalm 19:1-3 makes this very clear. **"The heavens declare the glory of God; the skies proclaim the work of his hands. Day after day they pour forth speech; night after night they display**

127

knowledge. There is no speech or language where their voice is not heard."

Watching a sunrise or sunset, anyone with an open heart would surely be moved to acknowledge the evidence of God's breathtaking workmanship. The beauty of these daily events in **"the heavens"** is consistent throughout the planet and throughout time. This shows that God creates easily accessible opportunities for all people, everywhere in every language, to learn of his existence and seek his glory every day.

Not only does God want knowledge of him available to all, God also wants all of us **"to be saved and come to the knowledge of the truth"** (1 Timothy 2:3-4). There is a false assumption that many people have about pagans (worshipers of false gods). It is assumed by many that if a group of foreign peoples do not know God, then this proves that God has not been involved in their life or that God is an uncaring God who shows favoritism. But this is unbiblical because **"...God does not show favoritism but accepts men from every nation who fear him and do what is right"** (Acts 10:34-35).

God is involved in all people's lives from the very beginning. He makes our individual spirit that we are born with (Ecclesiastes 12:7). And God doesn't just stop with our spirit, as seen in Psalm 139:13. **"For you created my inmost being; you knit me together in my mother's womb."** Not one person was created and given life without God. This is clarified even further in John 1:4 and John 1:9. **"In him was life, and that life was the light of men... The true light that gives light to every man was coming into the world."**

In Jesus we have life! We see that Jesus actually lights up everyone that comes into the world with the ability to be and to stay alive. Don't take it for granted. The sustaining force in your life is Jesus, whether you know it or not. Think of a baby, any little baby. I think of my daughter Anna when she was just born. She didn't have any discernable understanding of Jesus yet God made her super-cute. People were drawn to her. All babies have that quality. They are pure, innocent and radiant. Have you ever wondered why that is? It's because babies have the light of Jesus: they have just been lit up by God with pure life! Looking into the eyes of a baby, that innocence and the light of God is undeniable evidence of God's workmanship.

At some point in our development though, we lose that light due to the sin in our lives, since sin inevitably separates us from God, as put plainly in Isaiah 59:2. **"But your iniquities have separated you from your God; your sins have hidden his face from you, so that he will not hear."**

Thankfully, this grim reality is not necessarily the end of the matter. God always has a plan. During childhood, the plan for all kids includes the following from Matthew 18:10. **"See that you do not look down on one of these little ones. For I tell you that their angels in heaven always see the face of my Father in heaven."** So angels are assigned to look out for kids. Whether this is one-to-one observation, or each angel is assigned to ten kids is unknown, and frankly irrelevant. God knows how much protection is needed.

This angelic observation is not exclusive only to kids of Christian parents. Understand that you have had this protection in your youth and so will your children, whether you're a Christian or not. God's watchful plan is for all children. However, do not interpret this to mean that nothing bad can ever happen to our kids. (Don't we wish?) But know that those children who do pass away go to heaven. Jesus teaches this in Matthew 19:14. **"The kingdom of heaven belongs to such as these."** He's talking about the children.

Eventually though, these children grow up to join the crowd where **"...all have sinned and fall short of the glory of God"** (Romans 3:23). The majority grows to reject God even though the Bible explains that God's qualities are made known in creation, yet people reject God due to wickedness and their own suppression of the truth.

Romans 1:18-21 **"The wrath of God is being revealed from heaven against all the godlessness and wickedness of men who suppress the truth by their wickedness, since what may be known about God is plain to them, because God has made it plain to them. For since the creation of the world God's invisible qualities--his eternal power and divine nature--have been clearly seen, being understood from what has been made, so that men are without excuse. For although they knew God, they neither glorified him as God nor gave thanks to him, but their thinking became futile and their foolish hearts were darkened."**

This principle, of course, is for everyone, not just foreigners in remote pagan nations. If you reject God, your foolish heart is darkened and wrath comes to you. Asking a sincere question about people who never heard the gospel can be constructive, but it should not be used as an excuse to avoid following God. No one will have a valid excuse when God judges because God has made himself known through the very world we all live in. God is so evident that even birds, fish and animals know of God and that our life and breath is in his hands. Not only that, but these creatures would actually tell us so, if only we could understand them.

Job 12:7-10 **"But ask the animals, and they will teach you, or the birds of the air, and they will tell you; or speak to the earth, and it will teach you, or let the fish of the sea inform you. Which of all these does not know that the hand of the LORD has done this? In his hand is the life of every creature and the breath of all mankind."**

People who have never cracked open the Bible actually have more truth at their disposal than most people can imagine. Romans 2 explains that basic right and wrong (the Law) is written on the hearts of all people and that at the very least, we are judged according to the light that we have been given in our conscience.

Romans 2:12-16 **"All who sin apart from the law will also perish apart from the law, and all who sin under the law will be judged by the law. For it is not those who hear the law who are righteous in God's sight, but it is those who obey the law who will be declared righteous. (Indeed, when Gentiles, who do not have the law, do by nature things required by the law, they are a law for themselves, even though they do not have the law, since they show that the requirements of the law are written on their hearts, their consciences also bearing witness, and their thoughts now accusing, now even defending them.) This will take place on the day when God will judge men's secrets through Jesus Christ, as my gospel declares."**

God gives us many tools so that we can be respectful of his judgment. **"...He has also set eternity in the hearts of men..."** (Ecclesiastes 3:11). This concept of eternity set in our hearts is a built in radar sense that echoes in each of us something like, "I had better seek God and be good because forever is a long time, and my body won't last forever but my soul will. And I don't want to be punished for all the bad stuff I have done." That last thought is a killjoy. All of us deserve to be repaid for the evil we have done. Don't deceive yourself into thinking you are a good person because **"...No one is good--except God alone"** (Mark 10:18). What payment is due to us for our sin? Romans 6:23 states that **"...the wages of sin is death"** and if not for the grace of God, that would be the end of the story. We sin, our sin separates us from God, and then we die: game over.

Thank God that there is a way out and that he does not want us to go our own way, as exemplified in Acts 14:16-17. **"In the past, he let all nations go their own way. Yet he has not left himself without testimony: He has shown kindness by giving you rain from heaven and crops in their seasons; he provides you with plenty of food and fills your hearts with joy."**

We see here that part of God's testimony to us is the very food we have been eating for our entire life cycle. The Bible is saying that the very fact that we live in a world where there is food is proof of God's existence as well as evidence of God's kindness.

It is so encouraging to learn that while we are learning about God, no matter what stage in the understanding we're at, God is providing for us in multiple ways. He provides even for those who reject him.

John 1:16 **"From the fullness of his grace we have all received one blessing after another."**

Imagine a constant flow of blessings--a stream--continually coming to you. Most people do not view Jesus in this manner, but this is who he is. Streaming grace is what **"we have all received,"** whether Christian or not. It's because Jesus is absolutely loaded (**"from the fullness"**) with grace. Think of Jesus' grace as goodwill, kindness, and favor from an unseen source. It's like gifts from Santa Claus, the difference being that Jesus is real, all-powerful, giving every day, and often giving not based on how good you've been. That is love which only a true father can demonstrate: for the good and the bad.

131

Matthew 5:45 **"...He causes his sun to rise on the evil and the good, and sends rain on the righteous and the unrighteous."**

God makes the sun shine on you whether you deserve it or not, and whether you believe it or not. I have received good things so often in my own life as an undeserving, ungrateful, unbelieving fool. Yet still the sun shines bright, the rain makes the crops grow into food, I eat well, and it is all caused by God. What a great Father we have!

As our Father, God wants a relationship with us: not just any old relationship, but the best relationship at the best time and place. This is revealed in Acts 17:26-28. **"From one man he made every nation of men, that they should inhabit the whole earth; and he determined the times set for them and the exact places where they should live. God did this so that men would seek him and perhaps reach out for him and find him, though he is not far from each one of us. 'For in him we live and move and have our being.' As some of your own poets have said, 'We are his offspring.'"**

It takes faith to believe this: that God operates within our life so that we will seek him and best come to know him. All aspects of our life include what period we are born into, the exact places we live and our very movements and existence. I once thought it would have been better for me to have been born during the Italian Renaissance, but God knew better; that era was not the best time for me to come to know Jesus. God knew that 1998 in Illinois was best for me. And God was right! I trust him all the more for what he has done.

None of our life details are unknown or random to God. He is active in the entire human race, sustaining us and hoping that all the opportunities that we've been given to find him will not be wasted due to our own selfish, ungrateful and sometimes dull attitudes.

Think deeply about that last verse quoted from Acts 17:28. **"For in him we live and move and have our being...."** According to that statement, it is impossible to survive, exist, and move around without God. Without God we would all slump over in a lifeless and pathetic end. Yet how often do we operate as if we are completely independent and running on our own power? Such thinking is foolish and unbiblical. Human beings would cease to function without God.

To illustrate this point, imagine the coolest, latest smartphone with all the latest features, including a built in MP3 player, camera, video recorder, video calling, games, email, super-fast internet, long distance calling and even international calling. Now what good would that phone be if the power (battery) and the communications network (Verizon, AT&T) were taken away? It would no longer operate. It would be completely useless. It is the same with you and God. You are the device--the phone. God is the device maker, the power source, and the service provider. **"Do not think of yourself more highly than you ought..."** (Romans 12:3).

Unlike all worldly phone providers who operate under the unspoken motto, "Pay us or no service," God knows exactly how to balance mercy with judgment. Speaking of idolatry in Acts 17:30-31, Paul verifies God's will. **"In the past God overlooked such ignorance, but now he commands all people everywhere to repent. For he has set a day when he will judge the world with justice by the man he has appointed. He has given proof of this to all men by raising him from the dead."**

Obvious in this passage is that the entire world will be judged through Jesus: not Buddha, not the multitude of Hindu gods, not the multitude of other invented pagan gods, not your family, not your friends and certainly not you or me. Only Jesus will be the judge of us all, through his mighty word (John 12:48). Favorable judgment from Jesus and only Jesus means salvation. This is consistently stated in the Scriptures. As noted earlier Peter lays it out clearly in Acts 4:12, referring to Jesus. **"Salvation is found in no one else, for there is no other name under heaven given to men by which we must be saved."**

The narrow path to God's kingdom has a very specific plan to follow. The entry points are clearly marked out by Jesus in John 3:5. **"I tell you the truth, no one can enter the kingdom of God unless he is born of water and the Spirit."** It is obvious that Jesus considered the specific details of how to get into his kingdom as non-negotiable requirements. Therefore, if through the Scriptures, God says to be made into a disciple (Matthew 28:19), deny yourself (Luke 9:23), have faith (Colossians 2:12), make Jesus Lord (Acts 2:36), give up everything (Luke 14:33), have godly sorrow (2

Corinthians 7:10), repent (Mark 1:15), be baptized (Acts 2:38), and teach others to obey (Matthew 28:20), then those who want to be with God forever in paradise must take these commands seriously. Do not cut corners with the Lord. Shortcuts may work at the office, strolling through the woods, or with your household chores, but not with God. We must obey God's plan of salvation.

On a side note, keep in mind that this book is not an exhaustive study on conversion; if you want to become a Christian (and I hope you do), you need to be taught by a true Christian face to face.

Lingering Questions: Are You Still Doubting God?

After digesting and applying these life-changing truths, some lingering questions may pop into your mind. Herein, a few of the common ones will be addressed.

1) "Why doesn't God just force us to always seek him and love him? Then everyone would love him and no one would go to hell, right?"

I have had this very thought it the past, but the logic of this question is flawed. If someone is forced to love, then it's not love. Also think about the nature of a great father. A great father wants a freewill relationship with his children. And that's what God is: our Father (Luke 11:2). He doesn't force us to be with him. If God wanted that, he would just make a bunch of robots who would coldly obey his commands. But who would take pleasure from such a relationship? Rather, God wants us to choose to be with him out of our own freewill.

Think also of a marriage. If you were forced to marry a person that you had no desire for, where would the joy be? This would be a relationship of strife and oppression. Nobody wants that. Imagine what heaven would be like if it were full of people like that; it would not be a heaven. Rather it would be a population of depressed slaves still in bondage. That's not worship. Worship involves adoration. Healthy relationships must include seeking and choosing the one you love.

God knows this and shows it in John 4:23 where he is seeking true worshipers. **"...A time is coming and has now come when the true worshipers will worship the Father in spirit and truth, for**

134

they are the kind of worshipers the Father seeks." This mutual relationship is explained in Psalm 119:2 where we should be seeking him with fervor. **"Blessed are they who keep his statutes and seek him with all their heart."** It's a two way street. God is looking for people committed to him and we need to be looking with all our heart for God. If we do so, great promises await us, as described in Jeremiah 29:11-13. **"'For I know the plans I have for you,' declares the LORD, 'plans to prosper you and not to harm you, plans to give you hope and a future. Then you will call upon me and come and pray to me, and I will listen to you. You will seek me and find me when you seek me with all your heart.'"**

This reminds me of one afternoon, after I had just finished a prayer, my youngest daughter had a most profound question. This was immediately following my prayer of "God please help us to find more people who are open to the gospel, amen." My five-year-old daughter then asked, "Why doesn't God just **make** all the people come to church?"

This deep question led to a great discussion about how God wants us to freely choose him rather than for us to simply be cold, robotic followers. God wants a willing attitude in a willing relationship. I was amazed at how my daughter, at so young an age, was thinking on such a sound spiritual level, and I thank God for it.

2) "If God gave people free will, how can his disciples be predestined as it says in Romans 8?"

The word "predestined" is actually the Greek word "proorizo." That means "to predetermine, decide beforehand" (Thayer's Greek Lexicon). This question needs deeper analysis, because the idea of being predestined is hard to fathom outside of our own time period. The word "predestined" is in the Bible 4 times, including Romans 8:29-30. **"For those God foreknew he also predestined to be conformed to the likeness of his Son, that he might be the firstborn among many brothers. And those he predestined, he also called; those he called, he also justified; those he justified, he also glorified."**

The key to understanding this passage, and the concept of being predestined is grasping that God knows all things and he is bigger than time itself. In fact, he created time. That is why **"...with the Lord a day is like a thousand years, and a thousand years are like a day"** (2 Peter 3:8). From God's point of view, the beginning and the end are seen with the same ease that we might flip through the channels of a television or the pages of a comic book. Therefore God knows who ultimately chooses him and who doesn't. From God's almighty angle, it is supernatural predestination because he can exist outside of what we know as the passage of time. So he can decide beforehand (predestination) who has the right heart for him and how to orchestrate those lives for his appointed purposes.

However from our viewpoint, we have no idea what will happen next. Be grateful that God is **"the Beginning and the End"** (Revelation 21:6), and within that unfathomable time span, he is not merely watching from the sidelines and eating popcorn. **"For the eyes of the LORD range throughout the earth to strengthen those whose hearts are fully committed to him..."** (2 Chronicles 16:9). God is active in this life, and for the fully committed, an incredible destiny of strengthening awaits you in a future that to God is simply another point in time at his mighty fingertips. People who choose to have a great heart toward God *are* given an advantage in this life. This advantage is fair because it's available to everyone on an international level as God's eyes **"range throughout the earth."** Instead of getting bitter about this, just do what you know you need to do; cultivate your own heart to seek God with everything you've got and get **"fully committed to him."**

3) "Why does God say that he hated Esau before the man was even born? And why did God harden Pharaoh's heart (Romans 9:10-18)? Doesn't that show God as unloving and not allowing for freewill?"

As with the previous answer, much of this issue settles with the fact that God is not bound by time. He knows what choices you will make in the future. That's God's foreknowledge. For Esau and Pharaoh, too many of their adult choices went against God. Therefore, bitter consequences resulted. Let that be a warning to us all; if we are stuck in a cycle of repeated bad behavior, we may eventually hit the point of no return.

4) "The gospel has never been preached in all the remote corners of the world so God doesn't truly care for other nations since they never got the chance to hear the message, right?"

Wrong... The gospel already went out all over the world. Colossians 1:23 makes this very clear. **"...This is the gospel that you heard and that has been proclaimed to every creature under heaven, and of which I, Paul, have become a servant."** Way back in the first century AD, **"every creature under heaven"** had the gospel **"proclaimed"** to them.

See also Romans 10:17-18 where Paul writes, **"Consequently, faith comes from hearing the message, and the message is heard through the word of Christ. But I ask: Did they not hear? Of course they did: 'Their voice has gone out into all the earth, their words to the ends of the world.'"** This message does indeed go out to all the nations, as shown in Revelation 7:9. **"After this I looked and there before me was a great multitude that no one could count, from every nation, tribe, people and language, standing before the throne and in front of the Lamb. They were wearing white robes and were holding palm branches in their hands."**

137

This is a scene from heaven and it should build your faith that there are saved followers from every nation and tribe there.

People making uninformed assessments about who has or has not heard the gospel over time are merely guessing based on their extremely limited points of view. Only God has an accurate picture of who has heard the gospel throughout the ages. His command is to **"...Go into all the world and preach the good news to all creation"** (Mark 16:15). Jesus wants the gospel to go global and we need to obey that.

Some Christians get confused when they are challenged by non-believers to prove that the gospel has indeed gone global in the past. But there is no need to fall into this trap. We are commanded to **"make disciples"** (Matthew 28:19) in our lifetime, not investigate historical conversion rates or past missionary migration patterns. While the latter research may be fascinating, this is not our responsibility and is best left up to the only writer powerful enough to know: Jesus Christ. He keeps the names written in the book of life, not us (Revelation 21:27).

A sobering Scripture that helps to focus people back into their own time zone and own fate is Hebrews 9:27. Since **"...man is destined to die once, and after that to face judgment,"** no amount of after-the-fact guesswork will change the eternal outcome of those who have passed away before us. You can disagree with what the Bible says about people who don't walk with God, but that will not change the fate of the dead. Those sentimental about the death and eternal fate of a non-Christian loved one must eventually understand that **"God is a righteous judge"** (Psalm 7:11). What God decides is divinely correct, proper, and right! This means that God will not make a flippant or bad judgment call about any of our ancestors. They (and we) will all get what God decides they (and we) should get. Doesn't such determination take trust in God? We must. What God decides about people's eternity is the best and right decision. All people have opportunity for relationship with God. Whether they seek such a relationship is ultimately up to them. Those who don't seek God will suffer for it. The real issues is this: do you trust God with this reality?

If you don't trust God, you are in for a future of insecurity, confusion, and strife. Take some time to study the 87 times that the word "trust" appears in the Bible. Proverbs 3:5 is a great place to start. **"Trust in the LORD with all your heart, and lean not on your own understanding."** Memorize this verse and make it become your personal mission statement.

5) "Why didn't God just create and keep everyone in heaven to begin with and not even have an earth where people end up suffering?"

This sounds like an easy plan on the surface, but how quick are we to appreciate things that come easy? I frequently find myself acting ungrateful even for people in my own family because I assume (falsely) that they will always be there. This is sin and God can't have sin in paradise. By its very nature, heaven wouldn't be a heaven if it were a place full of sinful activity.

Think also of stereotypical rich kids who have everything but are still unhappy and/or total brats. They (and we) get that way due to their lack of gratitude for what they have. Not so with heaven, those in heaven will be grateful to be there because they have known suffering and appreciate that Jesus was sacrificed for them to have access to heaven. Jesus calls for persevering followers (not spoiled brats) who rise up for what is right to be with him in heaven. In Revelation 2:7 he says, **"To him who overcomes, I will give the right to eat from the tree of life, which is in the paradise of God."**

It comes down to how much you value your relationship with God. Do you value your relationship enough to overcome trials? God demands relationship with everyone who desires paradise. Access to paradise is a byproduct of relationship with God, not the end goal. Being close with God is the goal: that's relationship. Those who overcome the trials of this world because they greatly value their relationship with God are the ones who receive the privileges and citizenship of paradise.

6) "Aren't many remote jungle tribes closer to God since they live in nature and are less corrupted by the world?"

In the wild, people typically do not adopt the word of God as their standard because they're too busy surviving and holding on to their inherited manmade traditions. That's all about self and being deceived. The concept of the "noble savage" has been made popular by the entertainment industry, but the reality is that these peoples sin and fall short of God's glory just as all people do and so need forgiveness from Jesus (Romans 3:23).

7) "Since I don't believe that God is real, why are you trying to convince me that he exists?"

I get questions like this a lot. The short answer is "Because you still need God, whether you believe he exists or not." Some people try to shut your faith down by telling you that they are an atheist: that they do not believe in God. When a person says this, upon further inquiry, I have found that they are often lying and the real issue is that they are mad at God and simply do not want to talk about him. Therefore, when someone tells me they are an atheist, I remind them "It's a good thing that God still believes that you exist, because he created you."

For cases when a person truly doesn't believe that God is real, I will also try to ask a lot of questions like "How long have you held that opinion?" or "Was there ever a point when you did believe in God? If so, what has changed?" Those who respond to these questions with sincerity rather than a mocking tone may be more open to eventually getting together to study the Bible and listen to reason. Recounting my own conversion story also helps, since I was a former atheist too.

Another question to ask an atheist is "What do you think happens to you after you die?" If they say "Nothing," like a number of Chinese have told me, then I would start showing them the many scientific evidences that are in the Bible: things mankind could not have known at the time the Bible was written. For example, the book of Job, written about 1700 BC describes gravity thousands of years before it was discovered. In Job 26:7, God is the mighty one who **"suspends the earth over nothing,"** which is an accurate depiction of what gravity looks like from space: it looks like the planet is held up **"over nothing."**

See also the following verses for a longer study on how scientific findings continue to confirm the Bible: Numbers 19:11 regarding germs, Leviticus 17:10 regarding uncooked meat, Isaiah 40:22

regarding the shape of the earth, Job 36:27-28 regarding the water cycle, and Judges 13:3-4 regarding pregnant women not drinking alcohol. There are many more such Scriptures, yet this sampling alone should help anyone understand that the information in the Bible could not possibly have originated from the mind of man. Rather, **"men spoke from God as they were carried along by the Holy Spirit"** (2 Peter 1:20). After showing the person all these evidences, ask, "How could ancient people have known the answers to so many scientific realities that have confounded scientists until modern times?"

If an atheist says anything about their soul going to some unknown place after death, then another can of worms has just been opened. I would ask "Who created your soul?" or "Who created that unknown place?"

All these questions are designed to get the person thinking on a more spiritual level, and ultimately point them back to the mighty Messiah: Jesus Christ.

Not All Questions Need Answers Now

I have a lot of unanswered questions that I imagine God will explain in paradise. Part of maturity is understanding that we don't need to know everything. Rather we need to know what's essential to live life to the full. Trusting God is learning to live with limited knowledge.

Many of my questions would be most fascinating to have answers to. However, I must realize that can still function and even thrive without all the answers. In fact, I have to do so. For example, I was wondering about the nature of the cherubim that God posted to the east of the Garden of Eden to guard the way to the tree of life. That's from Genesis 3:23-24: **"So the LORD God banished him from the Garden of Eden to work the ground from which he had been taken. After he drove the man out, he placed on the east side of the Garden of Eden cherubim and a flaming sword flashing back and forth to guard the way to the tree of life."**

So many questions come to mind about the Garden of Eden and the expulsion of Adam and Eve:
- Are guards still posted outside the Garden of Eden?

- Do the guards look like the awe-inspiring cherubim described with great intensity in the book of Ezekiel? (See Ezekiel chapter 1 and 10)
- Did the guards like their job guarding the Garden of Eden? Was it a pretty slow job, with the world being sparsely populated? If it was a slow job, what would the guards do to pass the time? If the job was not a slow job, were the guards under constant attack from demons or other forces.
- Did Adam and Eve ever try to talk God or the guard into letting them back into the Garden?
- Were the animals kicked out too? Or did they stay there? If some animals did stay there, would they live forever? Also, if any of the animals stayed there, are they species that we have never actually seen before, perhaps like unicorns?
- Was a guard holding the flaming sword or was the flaming sword flashing back and forth in mid-air, propelled solely by the power of God?
- The New American Standard Bible, in Genesis 3:24, says that God **"...stationed the cherubim and the flaming sword which turned every direction to guard the way to the tree of life."** After reading this version carefully, could it mean that directions were actually "turned" in a supernatural manner, similar to the sort of hidden dimensions often imagined by fiction writers?
- Where is Eden now? Has Eden been transported off of Planet Earth to some heavenly location, or is it still on Earth yet the guards confuse or reroute anyone or any technology coming close to the location.
- In Revelation 2:7, the tree of life is **"in the paradise of God."** Does that mean that the Garden of Eden is another name for the paradise of God, or did God just move the tree?
- Did the serpent also eat the forbidden fruit as well? I ask because the serpent in the Garden is not mentioned as having eaten from the "tree of the knowledge of good and evil" when Eve and Adam ate from it.

- Unlike the "tree of life," which is mentioned a number of other times in the Bible, the **"tree of the knowledge of good and evil"** is not mentioned again after the expulsion of Adam and Eve. What happened to that tree? Will it be in paradise too? Or is there no need for it anymore?

I must realize that some of these questions might be trivial in the larger scheme of things, as in, "I just want to get to heaven and be with God face to face!" However, pondering on our origins and the ingenuity of our creator increases my faith, even without having all the answers. I liken such thoughts to the many times the prophets say to "meditate" on God's ways. Psalm 77:12 sums it up: **"I will consider all your works and meditate on all your mighty deeds."**

When it comes to unanswered spiritual questions, at the end of the day, I have to be completely fine with the reality of my limited knowledge. God knows everything. We don't. That's why he is God and we are not. This is all the more reason to seek relationship with our all-knowing master.

While we don't know everything, God does give his followers all the necessities, and we should be content with that, for that's a significant amount of giving. In 2 Peter 1:3, the apostle says that **"His divine power has given us everything we need for life and godliness through our knowledge of him who called us by his own glory and goodness."** Notice that Peter is saying that we have all we need through knowing the one who calls us. Jesus is the one who called Peter. Jesus is the one who calls us today. It's all about relationship with Jesus. If I trust God, then I must believe this statement; I have everything I need, as long as I continue to know Jesus. You don't need to know all the answers. You need to know Jesus.

Then you can help those who don't know him.

Bottom Line about People Who Never Heard of Jesus

In thinking about those who have never heard of Jesus, be assured that they have been given so much by God, as we all have. Those who never heard of Jesus have lives crafted by God in order to have opportunities to seek Jesus and be saved through him. Even in the most remote island, if there is someone seeking God, then surely God can do whatever it takes to get that person to the gospel. He can allow an earthquake to stir the inhabitants to evacuate to new lands and in the process, meet faith-sharing Christians. God can do anything: in fact, he can do **"immeasurably more than all we ask or imagine"** (Ephesians 3:20) to get people saved.

So while God is doing amazing things to get people on their knees and focused on him, his plan must also be understood as an interactive process. He entrusted his followers to take that message to the ends of the earth. If you claim to be a Christian, this means you. Get this message out; the words of Jesus (the Bible) will be the judge of all. Nothing but condemnation awaits those who reject Jesus, as his own statements confirm. **"There is a judge for the one who rejects me and does not accept my words; that very word which I spoke will condemn him at the last day"** (John 12:48).

These are strong statements. If you are hearing this message, don't delay to obey Jesus just because of unbelievers in a remote country that you don't even know. That's an empty excuse. The call rather is to get broken (godly sorrow) about your own sin, get faithful, get committed, get baptized, get forgiven and get on board with Jesus' plan to get trained and get fishing for lost souls. This way, the gospel gets out and many get saved.

Join the daily battle to make disciples of all nations. Once you do, that elusive question, "What about people who never heard of Jesus?" will no longer have to be a point of confusion for you. Your own conscience will be clear in knowing that God is using you to **"always be prepared to give an answer"** (1 Peter 3:15) and to seek and save the lost (Luke 19:10).

If you really care about people who have never heard of Jesus, do something about it! Show them the mighty Messiah. Don't be a dead end for the gospel or you'll wind up dead spiritually. Get on the narrow road that **"only a few"** find because it leads to eternal life (Matthew 7:14). You will meet people who've never heard of Jesus along the way, so take the initiative. Show them **"the way and the truth and the life"** (John 14:6). After all, no one comes to the Father except through Jesus the Christ, our mighty Messiah.

Chapter 17: Where Have All the Mighties Gone?

Pretend, for a moment, that you never read the Bible or any spiritual book. In that scenario, if I asked you what's the first thing that comes to mind when I say the word "mighty," what would be your response? Before I became a disciple of Jesus Christ, my answer would be "Mighty Mouse," the 1942 cartoon character created by Paul Terry. A younger generation may have answered "Mighty Morphin Power Rangers," or even "Mighty Ducks."

Regardless of your answer, mighty is not just a catchy adjective or a snappy title. In the world of today, mighty heroes have been largely replaced with silly heroes, and mostly fictional ones at that. Think of the ever-joking Spider Man, or Iron Man. In my own cartoon work, I too have been heavily influenced to create silly, disposable heroes that are here one moment, forgotten the next in a never ending parade of trivial pursuits.

Silliness aside, there must be mighty people out here today, right? Have they all died in combat, defending the country? Where have all the real life mighty men and women gone? All too often, real people have lost their sense of mightiness, but we can get it back. Only by returning to the mighty one who created us can we truly understand what mightiness is, and how we can participate in life with the strength that God provides. If your mind is straining to name someone whom you personally know who is mighty, then keep reading. There is much more to understand in the realm of mightiness. Set aside the mighty superheroes for what they really are: figments of someone's fleeting imagination. Forget the sports stars. Forget the movie stars who pretend to be mighty to make money. Turn your attention toward our mighty God. In doing so, you could be mighty too. How can this happen? First, a study on the word "mighty" is in order.

While fading as a word we use in popular conversation, the word "mighty" is used in the Bible 189 times. Today, "mighty" means "having or showing great strength or power" or simply "very great" (Source: Merriam-Webster Dictionary). This definition also can be applied to usage of the word "mighty" in ancient times, yet the ancient definition has a bit more fighting characteristics built into the to the word. The Hebrew word used for "mighty" in the Old Testament is "gibbowr." That word appears 158 times in the King James Version of the Old Testament and 131 of those times it is translated as "mighty" or "mighty man." However it is also translated in the Bible as strong (4 times), valiant (3 times), mighty ones (4 times), mighties (2 times), man (2 times), valiant men (2 times) and once each as strong man, upright man, champion, chief, excel, giant, men's, mightiest, and strongest (Source: Blue Letter Bible). In the New International Version of the Bible, "gibbowr" is also translated as hero, fighting men, or warrior.

Just from the word's usage, we see that "gibbowr" (mighty) is used to describe a desired characteristic of mankind. Who wouldn't want to be a hero, or valiant, or champion, or mighty? Of course, most importantly, and on a grand scale, this word is also used to describe a main characteristic of God.

God Is Mighty

Exodus 13:16 **"And it will be like a sign on your hand and a symbol on your forehead that the LORD brought us out of Egypt with his mighty hand."**

Not under wimpy circumstances, but **"with his mighty hand"** did God bring his people out of slavery. Not only is God mighty, and not only does he use that strength, but he wants us to remember the fact that he is mighty. The strong acts of God are to be **"a sign on your hand and a symbol on your forehead."** Consider the significance of these two body parts: you always see your hands, and everyone else always sees your forehead. In other words, God wanted the people to adopt visual cues to remind themselves and all others of his mighty rescue plan for them. God's mightiness is meant to be unforgettable. Is that how you think of your God? Make it so.

Isaiah 42:13 **"The LORD will march out like a champion, like a warrior he will stir up his zeal; with a shout he will raise the battle cry and will triumph over his enemies."**

We must stop picturing God as some falsely imagine: as a distracted deity swept away by the pleasures of paradise. Zealously involved in our existence, God has a fighting spirit to do battle for what is right. As **"a champion,"** the LORD will throw down his enemies.

Psalm 24:8 **"Who is this King of glory? The LORD strong and mighty, the LORD mighty in battle."**

Do you picture God as described above? He is **"mighty in battle."** God is a warrior, fighting for what is right. This quality of God gives me great confidence and security, because I follow him. God fights for what is right, and so must I. Despite this magnificent characteristic of God, I have stumbled, and have seen others stumble, when this fighting spirit of God is forgotten or downplayed.

How could fighting strength, such an obvious character trait of God, be so quickly cast aside by believers? Here are a few practical examples.

1) All Prayer, No Truth. You pray a lot but have very shallow, short, or infrequent individual times reading the Bible.

2) All Grace, No Truth. You identify with Jesus' merciful and peacemaking side, best displayed at the cross, yet you misinterpret this as a reason to rarely confront sin head on.

3) Wounded Warrior: You tried to fight for what's right in the past (and even fought hard) but became discouraged when things didn't go your way. Now you are tired and afraid to reengage in the battle due to unaddressed war wounds.

Have you fallen into any of these bad patterns? I have too. However, it's not too late to pick up your Bible--the spiritual sword-- and start swinging again for **"the LORD strong and mighty."** If you have lost your fighting spirit, be reminded that God is a champion warrior. Start fighting on his side. You cannot lose with him.

Jeremiah 20:11 **"But the LORD is with me like a mighty warrior; so my persecutors will stumble and not prevail. They will fail and be thoroughly disgraced; their dishonor will never be forgotten."**

God is not just associated with battle, he is **"a mighty warrior."** When you have a mighty warrior with you, doesn't it propel your sense of security? Those against God **"will fail"** in an unforgettable way. Verses like this accelerate my confidence to follow the LORD wholeheartedly. Persecutors lose. God wins.

Nehemiah 9:32 **"Now therefore, our God, the great God, mighty and awesome, who keeps his covenant of love, do not let all this hardship seem trifling in your eyes..."**

Here we find a depth to God's mightiness that often is not found in mighty men. God can be mighty (strong, brave, fighting, etc.) while also maintaining his loving characteristics. This is one of the hardest concepts for us to retain. Usually we see God as one or the other: a mighty fighter or a loving forgiver. The reality is that God is both, equally, in full measure. This trait of God can also be found it John 1:14, where Jesus is described as being **"full of grace and truth."**

Jesus is Mighty

It was prophesied that the Messiah would be a mighty warrior. This is one of the reasons that the people initially rejected Jesus. No one saw him wielding a sword or beheading giants like David. The Jews expected a powerful warrior king who would overthrow any opposing empire in a military campaign.

Psalm 89:19-20 **"Once you spoke in a vision, to your faithful people you said: 'I have bestowed strength on a warrior; I have raised up a young man from among the people. I have found David my servant; with my sacred oil I have anointed him.'"**

Here in Psalm 89, the Messiah is a sacredly anointed one who was clearly seen as one coming from the line of David with the strength of gibbowr: **"a warrior."** As we continue through some of the verses of this Psalm, we learn more exciting details about the Messiah.

Psalm 89:22, 45 **"The enemy will not get the better of him; the wicked will not oppress him.... You have cut short the days of his youth; you have covered him with a mantle of shame."**

In retrospect, it is understood with these two verses that despite oppression, Jesus did not stay defeated and dead. The wicked tried to oppress him and **"cut short the days of his youth,"** but it didn't stick. **"The enemy"** did **"not get the better of"** Jesus, and his resurrection proved it. In true heroic form, Jesus endured the shame of the cross and conquered death in order to offer his heart-level unity to us.

Psalm 89:50-51 **"Remember, Lord, how your servant has been mocked, how I bear in my heart the taunts of all the nations, the taunts with which your enemies, LORD, have mocked, with which they have mocked every step of your anointed one."**

We can be certain that this is about the cross because God's **"servant has been mocked."** Looking at all the people who mocked **"every step"** of God's **"anointed one"** on the way to the cross and even while hanging on the cross, this passage is a sobering reminder of how utterly rejected Jesus was by the Jews and Romans.

On a more personal note, Jesus was rejected by me as well, for all those years I refused to respond appropriately to the message of the cross. Thankfully, that did not stop the flow of God's faithful love to me through the sacrifice of the Messiah.

Psalm 89:24 **"My faithful love will be with him, and through my name his horn will be exalted"**

The Father's **"faithful love"** is with the Messiah. Faithful is reliable: we can count on the fact that God loves Jesus. Therefore we need to love who God loves: we need to love Jesus too! Thinking about all the amazing things Jesus did (and still does), he should be easy to love. Through the name of the Father, Jesus did mighty miracles during his ministry, and his name is still being elevated thousands of years later. **"Exalted"** (lifted up) on the cross, Jesus was lifted up from the tomb three days later. With the resurrections, 1 Corinthians 15:54 celebrates how death has been defeated by Jesus. **"Death has been swallowed up in victory."** No other mighty hero can match that.

Another example of one of Jesus' mighty miracles is predicted in Psalm 107:28-29. **"Then they cried out to the LORD in their trouble, and he brought them out of their distress. He stilled the storm to a whisper; the waves of the sea were hushed."** This prophecy was fulfilled by Jesus many centuries later in Mark 4:37-41. **"A furious squall came up, and the waves broke over the boat, so that it was nearly swamped. Jesus was in the stern, sleeping on a cushion. The disciples woke him and said to him, 'Teacher, don't you care if we drown?' He got up, rebuked the wind and said to the waves, 'Quiet! Be still!' Then the wind died down and it was completely calm. He said to his disciples, 'Why are you so afraid? Do you still have no faith?' They were terrified and asked each other, 'Who is this? Even the wind and the waves obey him!'"**

Note that in the ancient prophecy and its 1st century fulfillment, the people cry out to God during a terrible storm. These people are greatly distressed in both accounts. Then God completely calms the weather and the waves. Who do you rely on when circumstances get way beyond your ability to manage them? Mighty people must rely on Mighty God, or their own mightiness will soon be washed away.

Back to our examination of Psalm 89, we can see that Jesus can do all these amazing things because he has authority to do so. Psalm 89:27-29 **"And I will appoint him to be my firstborn, the most exalted of the kings of the earth. I will maintain my love to him forever, and my covenant with him will never fail. I will establish his line forever, his throne as long as the heavens endure."**

As a firstborn son, Jesus is appointed and lifted up with authority over all other authorities. Only through Jesus can we have access to this everlasting covenant which **"will never fail."** In view of this, we must bow down before the throne of Jesus, our warrior-king forever, fighting spiritual battles with endless love for us.

Men and Women Can Be Mighty

One of the most exciting characteristics of God's mightiness is that he also allows people to be mighty. We see this with the Messiah and we can see it with others too. Reading the Bible, we start to realize that these folks would have no chance at being mighty without God. This can best be seen in the life of Gideon.

Judges 6:11-12 **"The angel of the LORD came and sat down under the oak in Ophrah that belonged to Joash the Abiezrite, where his son Gideon was threshing wheat in a winepress to keep it from the Midianites. When the angel of the LORD appeared to Gideon, he said, 'The LORD is with you, mighty warrior.'"**

Gideon is basically hiding out when the angel comes to him and calls him a **"mighty warrior."** Yet he goes on to do amazing things for God. The key to his success is that he was made to understand that the source of his strength came directly from God.

Judges 6:36-37 **"Gideon said to God, 'If you will save Israel by my hand as you have promised--look, I will place a wool fleece on the threshing floor. If there is dew only on the fleece** and all the ground is dry, then I will know that you will save Israel by my hand, as you said.'"

In conversation with God, we see Gideon looking for assurances of victory through God. Gideon, the **"mighty warrior"** knows that God's backing is essential to his success. David also understood this, and he certainly passed this along to his mighty men.

2 Samuel 23:8 **"These are the names of David's mighty men: Josheb-Basshebeth, a Tahkemonite, was chief of the Three; he raised his spear against eight hundred men, whom he killed in one encounter."**

Eight hundred men are killed with a spear in one encounter: top that for mightiness.

2 Samuel 23:20-21 **"Benaiah son of Jehoiada was a valiant fighter from Kabzeel, who performed great exploits. He struck down two of Moab's best men. He also went down into a pit on a snowy day and killed a lion. And he struck down a huge Egyptian. Although the Egyptian had a spear in his hand, Benaiah went against him with a club. He snatched the spear from the Egyptian's hand and killed him with his own spear."**

Killing a lion in ancient times (without guns) under any circumstances is mighty, but willfully jumping down into a pit on a snowy day to kill a lion is utterly astonishing. The feats of David's mighty men are legendary, and whole books could be devoted just to them. Yet who could have done any of these things without God? No one, of course. But with our mighty God and his mighty Messiah, we can **"soar on wings like eagles... run and not grow weary... walk and not be faint."** (Isaiah 40:31).

1 Chronicles 12:18 **"Some Gadites defected to David at his stronghold in the wilderness. They were brave warriors, ready for battle and able to handle the shield and spear. Their faces were the faces of lions, and they were as swift as gazelles in the mountains."**

We see that God expanded the number of mighty men who came to David. Where are the mighties of this age? Who is brave today? Are the people in your church described as such: **"their faces were the faces of lions"**? Does this define you: bold character, confident, secure, strong, and brave? I believe that most religious people do not have these characteristics today because their faith and deeds are dead or dying on the vine (James 2:26). They have no real examples in their lives to walk with and imitate, and therefore become "mighty" in futile endeavors.

Isaiah 5:22 **"Woe to those who are heroes at drinking wine and champions at mixing drinks,"**

The word used in Isaiah 5:22 for "heroes" is "gibbowr." That is the same word used to describe David's mighty men. So it does matter what you become mighty in. Look at what too many people are "heroes" at today: drug addictions, video game or Internet obsession, impure thoughts/actions, living only for pleasure, overeating... the list goes on. Does any of this describe you?

The good news is that it doesn't have to be that way. The days of David's mighty men may have come and gone, but the days of Jesus' mighty men (and women) can be here right now, when more people repent of their sins. Then step out on faith by imitating Jesus with mighty deeds and working together for Jesus' purposes.

Yet how many Christians do you personally know who are truly mighty in this manner? Are you included in that number? If you are not feeling mighty and not being mighty, then you have to ask yourself: "Am I really walking with Jesus?"

In my own walk with Jesus, I have seen God move many people to mighty faith and deeds. These are people who are changing the face of the world. Men and women who had been abused have come to forgive their abusers. Almost dead marriages with a history of adultery have been revived with new life, better than ever. Cowards have become courageous. Liars have become lovers of the truth. Bored and bitter teens have become bold for the Lord. Unstable and depressed individuals find new hope in God's recovery plan, pressing forward to inspire the multitudes. People consumed with career and money have been transformed into reliable, compassionate parents. The greedy have become the biggest givers. Drug addicts get sober and move on to lead chemical recovery ministries. Gang members renounce filthy language, violence, and robbery to become positive role models--living examples of love. Selfish jerks who wouldn't think to give time and money to the poor become devoted to over a decade of charity work. Some of these scenarios describe me, and some of these scenarios describe those whom I have played a part in their mighty transformation by the guiding hand of God!

Remember always that the call to be mighty is not just an Old Testament charge. God is mighty, the Messiah is mighty, and today his people are called to **"be strong in the Lord"** through Jesus' **"mighty power"** (Ephesians 6:10). Known as the "Full Armor of God" passage, I will close with God's command for us to be "mighty" in the Messiah, and may we meet under the peace of our mighty God, yet clothed in his full armor.

Ephesians 6:10-18 **"Finally, be strong in the Lord and in his mighty power. Put on the full armor of God so that you can take your stand against the devil's schemes. For our struggle is not against flesh and blood, but against the rulers, against the authorities, against the powers of this dark world and against the spiritual forces of evil in the heavenly realms. Therefore put on the full armor of God, so that when the day of evil comes, you may be able to stand your ground, and after you have done everything, to stand. Stand firm then, with the belt of truth buckled around your waist, with the breastplate of righteousness in place, and with your feet fitted with the readiness that comes from the gospel of peace. In addition to all this, take up the shield of faith, with which you can extinguish all the flaming arrows of the evil one. Take the helmet of salvation and the sword of the Spirit, which is the word of God. And pray in the Spirit on all occasions with all kinds of prayers and requests. With this in mind, be alert and always keep on praying for all the saints."**

Appreciating that the full armor of God has been forged in time-tested truths about the Messiah is greatly encouraging. Let us wear this armor with understanding, depth, and honor.

Chapter 18: Most People Vote Jesus Is God

Jesus doesn't need your vote. But let me speak absurdly for just one paragraph to make a point. Perhaps those unsure of who God is would be swayed a little closer to the truth if everyone took a vote and declared that Jesus is God. Of course, people voting on who Jesus is will not actually change who Jesus is. However, it may nudge the doubters or the complacent toward their own discovery that Jesus is indeed God. Human beings are influenced by those around them. If the majority took a vote and acknowledged that Jesus is God, the naysayers and doubters would have one more reason to take Jesus seriously. At the very least, such a vote would influence people to find out what the big deal is about Jesus in the first place.

People would do well to acknowledge that so much about who Jesus is has already been given to and received by us in the Bible. This knowledge has spread to all sorts of people, whether they obey the Bible or not. In 1 Corinthians 4:7, the Apostle Paul poses a rhetorical question: **"what do you have that you did not receive?"** The answer, of course, is "nothing" because God either directly gives us what we have, or he allows us to receive it. Titus 2:11 sums up God's widespread offer of grace with this statement: **"For the grace of God, that brings salvation has appeared to all men."** John 3:27 confirms the giver/receiver relationship that we are all a part of: **"A man can receive only what is given him from heaven."**

Indeed, we have been given so much by the giver--our mighty God. Many people, including non-Christians, have been given the knowledge that Jesus is God. As explained in John 3:27, this insight has been delivered to us from heaven. I believe that many people also have been given at least a general knowledge that it is specifically in the Bible that the deity of Jesus is confirmed.

Wanting to test how far this general understanding permeates into our culture, I crafted a 1-question messianic research project. In a 2015 survey conducted online to an international audience as well as in person with Chicagoans, participants were asked to answer a loaded True/False statement about the nature of the Bible and the identity of God. The in-person surveys were conducted in Chicago neighborhoods known to be extremely diverse in religious beliefs: Rogers Park, Edgewater, and the South Loop. My son, Luke Chiappetta and I approached mostly strangers out in the community and asked them to answer our brief faith-related survey. The survey question was also posted online to a wide variety of internationally reaching websites, including gaming sites, pop culture groups, social media sites, as well as a few Christian-related sites. This survey was also emailed to over 400 of my contacts, most of whom are from the comics and publishing industry and not known to have a strong affinity toward any particular religion.

The question posed to all these people, in-person and online, went like this: *"True or False: The Old Testament accurately predicts that Jesus is God."* Participants could choose from 3 answers: True, False, or I don't know.

Survey Results

A total of **278** people responded to the 1-question survey. **173** participants answered "True, the Old Testament accurately predicts that Jesus is God." From this one statement, a number of spiritual insights can be extrapolated. A strong majority of participants believe that (1) the Bible contains accurate predictions, (2) that there is a God, and (3) his name is Jesus.

On the more concerning side, **78** people replied "False," that they did not believe the Old Testament to be accurately predicting that Jesus is God. One of these respondents also identified himself as an atheist, another even went so far as to call the Bible a work of fiction, and yet another person, famous as a pioneer in the comic book publishing industry, stated "I know the Old Testament predicts absolutely nothing." Such a statement is easily disproved. Even skeptics of the Bible who have studied the book admit that the Bible *predicts* many things, whether a person believes they were fulfilled or not.

One of the easiest Bible predictions to prove as fulfilled is in Genesis 22:17. God tells Abraham in about 2000 BC that **"I will surely bless you and make your descendants as numerous as the stars in the sky and as the sand on the seashore."** Counting all the

Jews who have existed over time as Abraham's physical descendants plus all the Christians that have existed since the 1st century (as Abraham's spiritual descendants), by now this number must be in the billions.

Back to the survey results, only **27** participants said they didn't know whether or not the Old Testament accurately predicted that Jesus is God. This was a surprising finding. In over 16 years of studying the Bible with people in the Chicago area, my personal encounters have revealed that most people know very little about what the Old Testament actually says. Therefore it was originally hypothesized in the design of this survey that the number of "I don't know" answers would be much higher.

For the in-person surveys, a second question was asked, regardless of the person's answer: *"Do you want to study the Bible?"* There were 35 people who responded to this second question. 20 participants said "Yes."

While over half of the in-person respondents said they wanted to study the Bible, so far only 1 of them actually scheduled time to do so. This is not so unusual. Most people have been followed up with at least twice and offered the opportunity to study. Some respondents may take longer to make Bible study a priority in their schedule. A few people, after I had simply told them that I was planning on conducting surveys about the Bible, commended me for what I was doing. For one of these people, it led to a great discussion about who Jesus is, and now that person is studying the Bible with me!

Research Conclusion

What can be concluded from this research? Most people believe that Jesus is God as predicted in the Old Testament and that the Bible contains truth in the form of predictions that came true. The majority of people vote for Jesus! That's good news.

However, from the in-person surveys, most people, even many who believe that Jesus is God, are not urgent to make time to actually study the Bible. Moreover, a significant minority of people do not believe the prophecies about Jesus in Bible or don't know what it says.

On a personal note, wading through so many different opinions (especially the harsh and negative ones in the online gaming forums) was challenging. Yet it helped me to remember how lost I was before I came to understand and apply the Scriptures to my life. Having a patient attitude as I interacted with people and their opinions is very important. What helps me is remembering that God loves people, and wants all **"to be saved and to come to the knowledge of the truth"** (1 Timothy 2:4).

I view this survey as not just a data gathering exercise, but also a seed planting operation. So I need to respect people, and love them no matter how they react: right, wrong, kind, or rude. Isn't that what Jesus did at the cross? People need to know who their Messiah is, and I strive to be a person who draws people closer to Jesus, not repulses them away in an arguing contest. Many decades ago, I was one of those harsh, rude arguers myself. Yet God and his people were patient with me.

Truth seekers are certainly out there. Recently, in our north side Chicago ministry, a talented personal trainer who was raised in the USA with almost no knowledge of Jesus just became a Christian. Also exciting, 5 people from Mongolia are studying the Bible with us and want to become part of God's kingdom as well. As Jesus says in Matthew 9:37-38, **"...the harvest is plentiful, but the workers are few. Ask the Lord of the harvest, therefore, to send out workers into his harvest field."** What's needed is more workers (real Christians) to go out and tell more people about Jesus as they walk his walk. That is what I am asking God to give us: faithful workers. My hope and prayer is also that God, as the great giver, will open up more minds to give them a heart to learn who Jesus is: our mighty Messiah, our mighty God.

Bonus Fun Chapter: Messianic Minecraft

Everything significant that I wanted to share at this time about *Mighty Messianic Prophecy* has been written about in the many previous chapters of this book. The academic and scholarly research portion of this work is now officially over. Now it's time for some random, yet also surprisingly spiritual fun as we think more about the Messiah in unconventional, yet still respectful ways.

When someone mentions videogames, usually the last thing a person thinks about is reverence for God or even spiritual growth. This is quite understandable, since I have studied the Bible with many people who eventually confess that the reason they lead such undisciplined lives is due largely to their excessive devotion to time spent playing video games. Some even call it an addiction. Nevertheless, my hope with this bonus material below, is to slightly alter such a perspective--at least as it relates to something that I like to call "Messianic Minecraft."

As a mini-history lesson, Minecraft is a popular videogame created by a Swedish programmer. It debuted in 2009. It falls under the Open World category of videogames, because each player gets to explore and reshape their own world. As of this writing, over 35 million copies of the game have been sold. Would it surprise anyone to learn that it was campus students/gamers at church who first introduced this easy to use game to me and my kids? My son took to the simple building aspects of game immediately, but it took a while before it grew on me and my youngest daughter.

There is something fascinating and inspiring about the ability to mimic God's ability to create, reshape, and even destroy things at will. Since we are made in God's image, as it says in Genesis 1:27, I do believe that we have a built in desire to imitate our maker and be creative ourselves. The game of Minecraft and its mobile version, Pocket Minecraft, allow users to do such things virtually and with relative ease.

On a cautionary note, an out of the-box copy of Minecraft is not entirely a beacon of purity. It certainly seems like it at first, though. A user creates things from an inventory of over 300 items, and most of them are common construction items. The vast majority of these items are typical building materials (stone, wood, sand, glass), plus a variety of tools (shovels, pickaxe, swords), as well as the ability to create plants and creatures (animals, villagers).

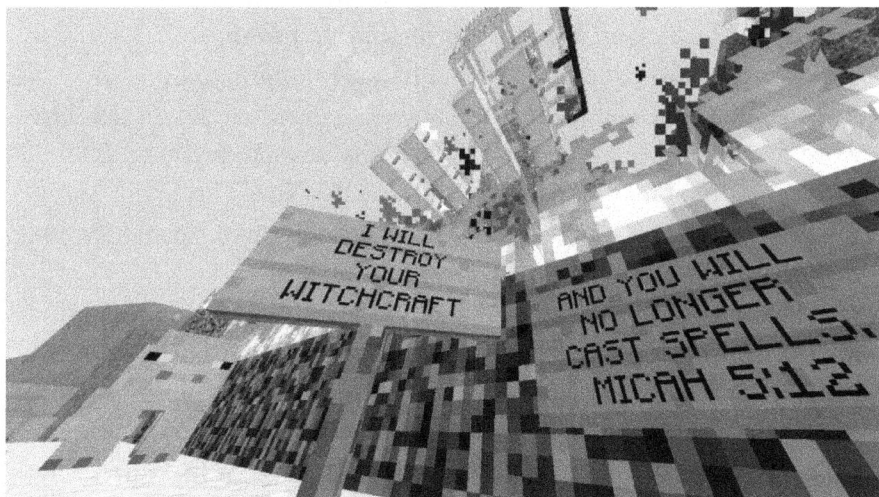

However I was disappointed to discover that also built into the game are a few witchcraft-related items that I have taught the kids to steer clear of, even though it's just a videogame. These sorcery related items include potions, an enchantment table, and the ability to "spawn" witches. As long as a player doesn't go into the inventory to use these specific items that represent sorcery elements, then the witchcraft component of the game remains largely inactive.

While a large portion of the world has been completely desensitized to sorcery in popular media (Magic the Gathering card game, Harry Potter, etc.) and thinks such influences are harmless or even cool, the Bible has much to say against sorcery. Simply put, it is evil and incites the wrath of God.

Deuteronomy 18:9-14 **"When you enter the land the LORD your God is giving you, do not learn to imitate the detestable ways of the nations there. Let no one be found among you who sacrifices his son or daughter in the fire, who practices divination or sorcery, interprets omens, engages in witchcraft, or casts spells, or who is a medium or spiritist or who consults the dead. Anyone who does these things is detestable to the LORD, and because of these detestable practices the LORD your God will drive out those nations before you. You must be blameless before the LORD your God. The nations you will dispossess listen to those who practice sorcery or divination. But as for you, the LORD your God has not permitted you to do so."**

Clearly we are directed by God to have nothing to do with sorcery. It is "detestable" to God, and not permitted. So let that be a word of warning to proceed very carefully around anything with even a hint of sorcery. Also forbidden in the New Testament, the following account of how the first century church in Ephesus viewed sorcery is also quite helpful and even convicting.

Acts 19:18-20 **"Many of those who believed now came and openly confessed their evil deeds. A number who had practiced sorcery brought their scrolls together and burned them publicly. When they calculated the value of the scrolls, the total came to fifty thousand drachmas. In this way the word of the Lord spread widely and grew in power."**

A drachma was a silver coin worth about a day's wages. Think about how much money that would be. These former sorcerers would have to collectively work 50,000 days to make that money back. This account doesn't specify how many people burned their scrolls, but let's guess it were 50 people. These 50 people would have to work every day for almost 3 years to make up for those lost wages. While the world highly valued these scrolls of sorcery, the disciples of Jesus burned them up in repentance before God.

Back to a discussion on the Minecraft universe, playing Minecraft (without the witchcraft components), most users simply construct and destroy almost whatever they want in a Lego-like universe of their own design. I have played the game in a slightly atypical manner and have come to rename it "Messianic Minecraft." For those who may need a reminder, the word "Messiah" means "anointed one" in Hebrew, with "Christ" being the Greek translation of 'Messiah." Therefore, anything divinely messianic has to do with Jesus Christ. In the case of Messianic Minecraft, I write Scriptures onto the various blocks and corners of this virtual world. The verses copied all have to do with the coming of the Messiah who has been prophesied about from the beginning of time: Jesus Christ.

Ironically, in the back-end structure of the game, the various worlds a player can make in Minecraft are called "saves." That's even the exact name of the folder where all the different worlds a user creates are stored: in a file folder called "saves." While Messianic Minecraft (or any other kind of Minecraft world) won't actually save anyone, in Messianic Minecraft, the game environment certainly celebrates the saving power of the Messiah--Jesus Christ.

Playing the game, I have found myself constructing and exploring while discovering powerful Scriptures that I have copied onto the walls and unique places of this cyber-generated universe. It's a place where I have reinforced my faith in fun as I've beefed up my knowledge of God's word along the way. For visual learners such as myself, I see it as a great way to help memorize Bible verses while feeding the urge to play at the same time.

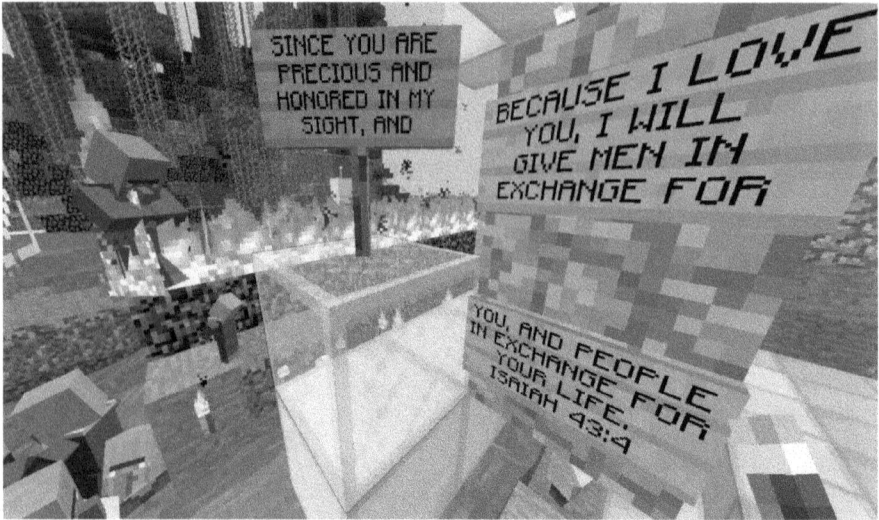

SINCE YOU ARE PRECIOUS AND HONORED IN MY SIGHT, AND

BECAUSE I LOVE YOU, I WILL GIVE MEN IN EXCHANGE FOR

YOU, AND PEOPLE IN EXCHANGE FOR YOUR LIFE. ISAIAH 43:4

After spending most of my life as a pretty artsy person, I have come to an insight about the creative process. In the past I thought that creativity was what fed my soul. Now I understand that God does the feeding. **"Man shall not live on bread alone, but on every word that comes from the mouth of God"** (Matthew 4:4). In the short term, being creative is almost always fun, yet the sense of creative accomplishment can be fleeting--here today, gone tomorrow--and soon there's pressure to create something new again. The cycle never ends. It leaves you constantly hungry, but never full.

FORGET THE FORMER THINGS; DO NOT DWELL IN THE PAST.

SEE, I AM DOING A NEW THING! NOW IT SPRINGS UP; DO YOU NOT

PERCEIVE IT? I AM MAKING A WAY IN THE DESERT AND STREAMS IN

THE WASTELAND. ISAIAH 43:18-19

Jesus fills the hunger of the soul. Ever since I have come to know him, I appreciate the creative process more. The fulfillment of being able to create something is richer when I humbly acknowledge that God has given me the tools to be creative as an extension of his own

166

creativity. People should use their abilities to give God the glory in all that they do, and bring as many people as possible along for the ride. It's not about what I can't do; I can't really create a universe-- virtual or otherwise. It's about what I can do; I can create situations that inspire people to follow the ultimate creator: God. In fact, we can all do that, and we all should.

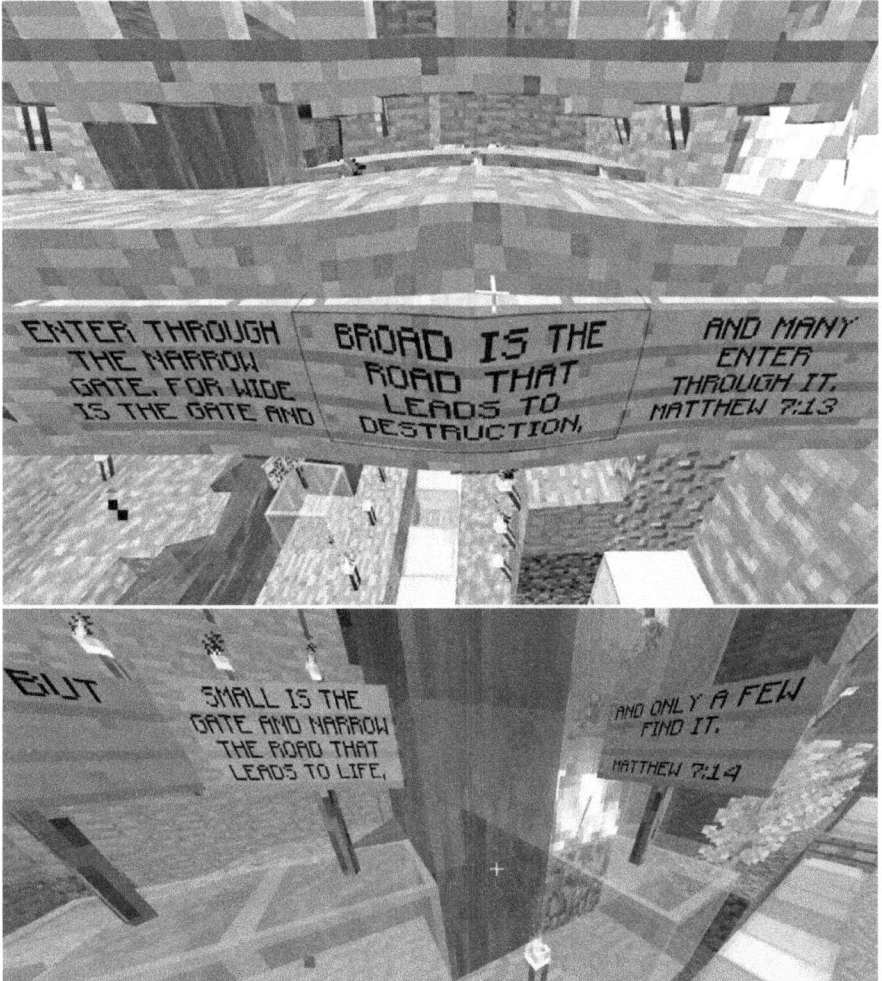

I think we all have some originality to us that God gave us as a gift. Sadly, so many in the world strive to be so unique that they run from God in search of someone or something new. It's quite common: many hop on the broad road full of other rebels competing unnecessarily with each other for personal awesomeness. That's a crowded yet alienating existence. Some folks get insecure because they don't stand out or feel that they are not unique enough. Yet there's nothing wrong with not being super-unique. Many people act so weird all in the name of being unique. People should stop trying to draw attention to themselves and learn to be who God is calling them to be through his mighty word. Then they can be secure in drawing attention to God with the creativity he has given all people.

Conversely, we also have certain things that we copy from others--characteristics that are not at all unique--and that's fine. From King Solomon to the artist Picasso, creative and talented types have alluded to the fact that people copy off of those who came before them. Read what Solomon says about newness in Ecclesiastes 1:9, **"There is nothing new under the sun."** What Picasso is attributed to have said was that "Good artists borrow, great artists steal."

To me, the real take-away lesson about how to use creativity is that imitation and modelling what already works are part of our God-given collective human experience. Philippians 4:9 is one of the many places that gives a biblical thumbs-up to godly imitation. **"Whatever you have learned or received or heard from me, or seen in me--put it into practice. And the God of peace will be with you."** When we create (conscious of it or not), we are expressing our desire to be like our Father in heaven, who is the ultimate creator whom none can surpass. Let's give honor to God with our creations and experiences.

One of my favorite Scriptures is 2 Samuel 14:14 which speaks to God's huge heart of compassion for people in trouble--even those in the sorry state of banishment. The wise woman from Tekoa said to King David, **"Like water spilled on the ground which cannot be recovered, so we must die. But God does not take away life; instead he devises ways so that a banished person may not remain estranged from him."**

God has devised ways to rescue; isn't that comforting? That verse is not only encouraging for all who might feel like they have ended up in the dog house of this life. The passage may also be a messianic prophecy about how Jesus was rejected by the people and condemned to die. That's beyond banishment. Yet God the Father devised the way for Jesus to **"not remain estranged from him."**

Therefore, I do believe this to potentially be a prophecy about the resurrection. The direct context is in reference to Absalom, who was the banished son of David at the time that the woman of Tekoa was speaking to King David. Not coincidentally, Jesus is also referred to numerous times in the New Testament as the son of David.

If this Scripture is not a prophecy about the resurrection, at the very least, it shows God's amazing mercy and love--always willing to go the extra mile to save us.

While very fun and creative, Messianic Minecraft, or any other video game, certainly can't replace deep bible study: don't even think about it. However, as a lighthearted supplement, wouldn't it be nice to play games while picking up eternal nuggets of truth as well? My hope is that we all become addicted, not to videogames, but to the Mighty Messiah. Such is the intent that has been stacked up in the strange yet remarkable cubes of Messianic Minecraft.

About the Author

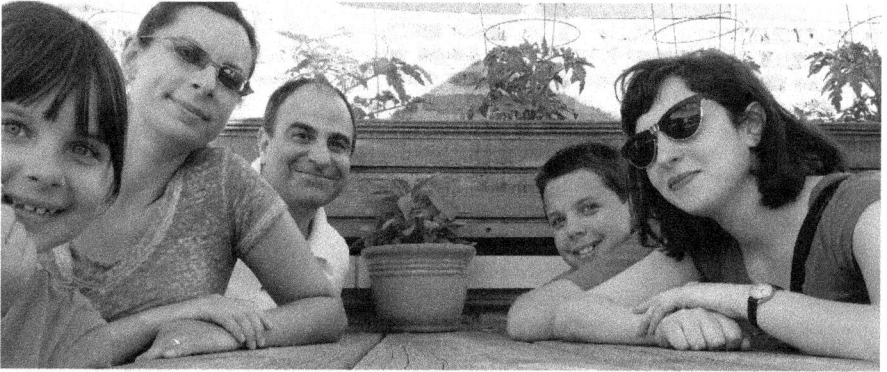

Renaissance man might be the best way to describe Joe Chiappetta. He is an Author, Cartoonist, Painter, Photographer, Pastor, Publisher, Community Organizer, Researcher, Choir Singer, and Trainer.

As the author of 5 full length nonfiction books, 5 full length fiction books, as well as numerous magazines and articles, Chiappetta has won many awards. This includes an Illinois Arts Council Award for the project: "Back Pain Avenger/Disability in Comics." The book, research, and speaking tour surrounding the Award focused on issues of disability in the history of comic books, as well as presenting a non-medicated memoir of rehabilitation. Joe is also a seasoned photographer, with his photos appearing in many of his publications and training courses.

For his family documentary work on the graphic novel "Silly Daddy," Joe was the recipient of the Xeric Award as well as numerous other award nominations over the years. Chiappetta is a husband and father of three who loves God and bicycle riding.

Since 1999 Joe has been leading community Bible discussion groups in the Chicago area. He's one of the founding members of the Chicago International Christian Church and leads both members and non-members in areas of applied Christianity, parenting, marriage, service to the poor and those with disabilities, and mental health issues.

Joe is the Director of MERCYWORLDWIDE's Chicago Branch, which is part of a global nonprofit charity. Chiappetta increased the scope of this organization from annual to monthly service projects helping people with disabilities whose families are no longer involved in their lives. Every month, he leads teams of volunteers into the group homes of Chicagoans with disabilities for MERCY Family Time: an evening of playing games, singing, and building family with those who are often forgotten by society.

Joe is also the founder of Chicago's Workforce Developer Network (WDN). It's the oldest collaborative of organizations working together to place more people with disabilities in jobs. In 2014, Joe successfully negotiated the restructuring of WDN to be a key program of MERCYWORLDWIDE. This increased awareness for Chicago's Network and promoted the employment of people with disabilities on a national scale. In this same year, employers hired 137 people with disabilities through WDN, which generated nearly $2 million in benefits to society.

Joe received a Bachelor of Arts in Charity Services from the International College of Christian Ministries in Los Angeles. He's also an alumni of Northern Illinois University with a Bachelor of Fine Arts who graduated cum laude and received the Dean's Award. His interdisciplinary education and experiences have encouraged him to use creativity combined with integrity to live a meaningful life to the full.

For a complete list of available books by Chiappetta, go to **www.joechiappetta.blogspot.com**

www.ingramcontent.com/pod-product-compliance
Lightning Source LLC
Chambersburg PA
CBHW071534040426
42452CB00008B/1007